Remember my 3 best
friends.

with E.Kaurianon. you

FDNY - EMS

NYTF - 1

D1110641

The Downwind Walk

A USAR Paramedic's Experiences after the
Terrorist Attacks on September 11, 2001

Steve Kanarian, EMT-P, MPH
FDNY EMS Lieutenant (Retired)

authorHOUSE®

AuthorHouse™
1663 Liberty Drive
Bloomington, IN 47403
www.authorhouse.com
Phone: 1-800-839-8640

First published by AuthorHouse 10/3/2011

ISBN: 978-1-4567-9889-5 (sc)
ISBN: 978-1-4567-9887-1 (e)
ISBN: 978-1-4567-9888-8 (dj)

Library of Congress Control Number: 2011915820

Printed in the United States of America

This book is printed on acid-free paper.

Because of the dynamic nature of the Internet, any web addresses or links contained in this book may have changed since publication and may no longer be valid. The views expressed in this work are solely those of the author and do not necessarily reflect the views of the publisher, and the publisher hereby disclaims any responsibility for them.

The stories in the book were compiled from the memories of the author, who was a paramedic serving at Ground Zero, and the EMTs and paramedics he knew. An effort was made to tell as accurate a history of these events as they are remembered. In some cases fictional names were used and any similarities to living people are purely coincidental.

Photographs

Acknowledgements

I want to express my sincere gratitude to my wonderful colleagues who generously gave me permission to write about their life experiences and to include their pictures. I want to thank Joe Conzo, Pat Bahnken, Kevin Cassidy, Keith Mcgregor and Domenic Maggiore for sharing their experiences with me. I also want to thank my family for their continued support and my co-workers from Battalion 55 such as Captain Santo, Booch, Mike Condon and others who made dealing with 9/11 bearable.

I would like to extend my appreciation to Bob Reeg and Peter Kearny who survived the Collapse of the world Trade Center and Paramedic Bill McCabe who was in the Trade Center in 1993 when it was bombed. I appreciate your friendship and appreciate your presence, you are my "Good" Trade Center stories.

I appreciate the unqualified support Jason Hums gave me through phone calls in the hours after 9/11 and the years following that event. I would like to thank Kevin Bachi for his support in writing this book and packing his bags the morning of September 11, 2001 to come find us.

I would like to thank Chief James "J. P." Martin, of the FDNY EMS, for allowing me to tell his story and whose interest in this project validated the concept of this book. I would also like to thank Christine Alvarez, Director of EMS Education at LaGuardia Community College, for her insightful support during this endeavor. I also want to thank Anne Castioni, Sam Bradley, Caroline Osborne and Dr. Maureen Sowa for taking the time to review the draft version of this book and sharing their insights, and Dr. Mary Zahm for her assistance in preparing the manuscript for publication.

I would also like to thank Scott Meahger who started me on my EMS career, and David Drowne of the Rehoboth Rescue Squad who gave me the heavy rescue and rope rescue training that enabled me to be selected for the New York City Urban Search and Rescue (USAR) team. I also would like to thank the many instructors at the NYC EMS Academy who trained us in safety, bloodborne pathogen and terrorism awareness training throughout the years.

I would like to thank Chief's Walter Kowalczyk and Steven Kuhr for their influence and the expertise they passed on to me in MCI management. I appreciate the superior training I received through Deputy Chief Paul Maniscalco and the New York City Fire Department Special Operations Command who provided us with the finest collapse rescue, confined space, rope rescue and Haz Mat training, which helped us to work safely on September 11, 2001. I would also like to thank Doctor Dario Gonzales who foresaw what lay ahead and trained us for this eventuality.

I appreciate the dedication of Chief Maniscalco, Chief Charlie Wells, and Chief Carl Tramantana who ensured that we had the best training from the best resources in New York City. I would also like to thank Chief James P. Booth who kept us focused on those long nights at Ground Zero as hope rapidly slipped into the horizon. Writing a book is a tremendous endeavor that cannot be accomplished alone. Writing a book about 9/11 is an especially difficult task. I am very grateful for the assistance of those mentioned above who helped make this book a reality. I had a burning need to share this story about the role of EMS in the rescue operations following the bombings of the World Trade Center on September 11, 2001, including the steps that my "three best friends" and I took to stay safe and healthy while working at Ground Zero.

I would especially like to acknowledge the sacrifice and understanding my wife Moira and my three children showed me during those stressful months. Unfortunately we often give our all at work for our patients and we have little left for our family when we return home. I will spend the balance of my life trying to atone for time lost.

I would like to thank my mother Mary Kanarian Zahm for supporting my career and writing. I am especially appreciative of my father Peter Kanarian who taught me the value of people and how to work tirelessly until the job was done, completely done. I also wish I was able to express my understanding to my Uncle Norire Kanarian who suffered from stress following World War Two combat in the South Pacific. I now know why you were so sad on holidays. May you rest in peace, with pride.

Thank you to all listed above and those countless co-workers and friends who had a hand in shaping my abilities and keeping me motivated when the going was exceedingly tough as well as those whose names I may have inadvertently omitted.

I am especially grateful for the many people I have worked along side of who supported me along the journey. When asked if I miss the work in retirement I reply, "No, but I do miss doing important jobs with great people."

Dedication

I dedicate this book to all of the EMTs and paramedics who took the downwind walk on September 11, 2001 in the aftermath of the terrorist attacks on the World Trade Center in New York who continue to live with the memories of this tragic event.

I also dedicate this book to the memory of those EMTs and paramedics who died on September 11, 2001 or in the months and years following their exposure at Ground Zero. I have written this book with these EMTs and paramedics in mind.

I have written this book with the younger generation of EMS rescuers in mind because I want them to know what their brothers and sisters experienced on September 11, 2001 and how we survived serving at Ground Zero.

Foreword

By
Dr. Chris Nollette, NREMTP, LP, Director
Ben Clark Training Center/Public Safety,
Moreno Valley College, Riverside Community College District

*T*he Downwind Walk: A USAR Paramedic's Experience after the Terrorist Attacks on September 11, 2001* is a unique look through the eyes of a fellow brother who took that downwind walk for the rest of us during that fateful day. It is a professional and personal account of what transpired shortly before and during one of the most painful and tragic events of our history.

The author, Lt. Steve Kanarian, not only has an incredible vantage point as an EMS professional in one of the most prestigious departments in our country but also as a fellow EMS educator he brings an additional perspective to these horrific events. Always a leader, EMS professional, and a consummate EMS educator, this book is another chance to teach the next generation the importance of friendship, teamwork, a love for ones profession and for mankind.

He understood that he was a part of history and that the next generation can learn from the terrible events that unfolded on America's sad day. Lt. Steve Kanarian and I spent many hours talking about the how similar our professional sacrifice can be compared to the sacrifice of the 300 Spartans as they locked their shields against the invading army led by Xerxes, King of Persia in 480 B.C. at the narrow pass at Thermoplyae.

Maybe the shield of today is the patch that we wear on our shoulder or the badge on our chest. Only a Spartan can tell you what drives them forward — shoulder to shoulder with their brothers and sisters — in the face of great danger and personal sacrifice. Only a Spartan can know how important their service is to their fellow soldiers and the cities that they protect. Only a Spartan can accept death for another without stepping back or to the side meeting death face-to-face.

Steve Kanarian and the men and women who locked shields together on that day know the answer of why they do it. We are blessed as a nation to have Spartans among us whose sacrifice becomes our greatest inspiration and our greatest teacher of how to live our lives and how to live our profession.

They weren't there, they went there. They didn't run from the fire, they ran into the fire. They didn't run down the staircases, they ran up the staircases. They didn't lose their lives, they gave them.

Lt. Col. Dave Grossman

Foreword

By
Christine Alvarez, Director of EMS Education
LaGuardia Community College

A tall lean man of few words, Joe Farrell is well respected among his fellows at the NYS Office of the Bureau of EMS. On September 11, 2001, Joe responded to the World Trade Center only to find the building crashing down around him. Seeking refuge from the falling concrete and steel, he spied two FDNY fire trucks nearby and dove under one of them. When he emerged, he saw that although the truck he had chosen had left him unscathed, the other truck's tires had all blown out and the two-ton truck had pancaked onto the ground.

Manuel "Manny" Delgado, is a man of great integrity and inner strength. An experienced paramedic from the FDNY Office of Medical Affairs, he likewise responded to the World Trade Center only to barely escape with his life. As he approached the Towers, he acknowledged his former student James "Jimmy" Pappageorge as he entered the Trade Center. Soft spoken Jimmy had just recently left EMS for the "fire side" of FDNY and was one of the 343 firefighters who perished that day. Prior to the buildings' collapse, victims in the flaming towers were tragically jumping or falling to their deaths. This caused unbelievable physical and psychological trauma for those on the ground. The people and debris falling from the crumbling Towers missed Manny by only inches.

Paramedic Enrique Gonzalez was triaging patients in a building adjacent to the Towers when the walls began to shake. The EMS Lieutenant wisely ordered all to immediately evacuate the premises. That order was countermanded by a Fire Captain who admonished them to follow their orders to triage in that location or be subject to disciplinary charges. Thankfully all survived as Enrique and the other brave responders evacuated their patients and personnel minutes before the structure fell.

Captain Kathy Mazza-Delosh was not so fortunate. A former operating room nurse and current EMT Instructor, Kathy held the position of Commander of the Port Authority Police Academy at the time of the attacks. She responded to Ground Zero with other courageous members of the Port Authority. For a long time no one knew what had happened to her. Her husband, family, and friends hoped she could have somehow survived the Towers' collapse. As the painstaking work of removing the debris took place, eventually her remains and her story were revealed. She had died evacuating a disabled woman together with another Port Authority Police Officer. Her gun was empty of bullets as she had used her weapon to shoot out the lobby windows to open further opportunities for victims to escape.

I have shared with you briefly the exceptional bravery and service of these five individuals within our emergency services. As you take *The Downwind Walk* with Paramedic and former Lieutenant Steven Kanarian, he will take you into the inner world of EMS especially in the days of and after the WTC attacks. The danger at Ground Zero extended well beyond September 11 in part due to mountains of unstable debris and raging underground fires. Later would come the respiratory diseases and psychological trauma. Steve will share with you his experiences as they came from around the country to help in the search for survivors. He will share with you THE REALITY of those on the street.

In *The Downwind Walk*, Paramedic Kanarian brings us back to that time when we felt together as a community, vowing NEVER TO

FORGET all those who passed away on or because of the September 11 attacks from the Pentagon, to Flight 93, to the Twin Towers.

There are so many stories we still do not know. Learn from this one.

About the Book

The Downwind Walk: A USAR Paramedic's Experiences after the Terrorist Attacks on September 11, 2001 lets you experience the tragic events following the terrorist attacks on the World Trade Center in New York on September 11, 2001 through the eyes of an Urban Search and Rescue (USAR) paramedic who went into harm's way to rescue the victims, which rapidly included many of his brothers and sisters of the Fire Department of New York (FDNY) and New York City Emergency Medical Services (EMS).

The author was a member of the FDNY EMS Command in the Bronx who Supervised EMTs and paramedics who responded to the attack on the World Trade Center. Steven Kanarian went downwind with the USAR team to take a first hand look at that mass casualty incident (MCI), assess the damage and losses, and rescue those lost in the terrorist attack. Take the downwind walk with Steve Kanarian as he recounts the events, sights, smells and vivid memories of that unforgettable September ... from eye level at Ground Zero, in his dusty boots.

In this book, you will read stories about EMTs and paramedics who were at Ground Zero with the author, including some who were wounded or traumatized and others who made the "ultimate sacrifice." You will also learn about EMS personnel who made a significant contribution to patient care and public service by responding to numerous 911 calls or assisting fallen coworkers that week despite extremely stressful working conditions.

No doubt you have heard the popular stories that tell of heroism on airline flights, in the Twin Towers and at the Pentagon. It is also important for future generations of Americans to know about the sacrifice and dedication of EMS first responders. Now is the time to share their stories on the 10th Anniversary of 9/11.

Steve Kanarian wants future EMTs and paramedics to know about the individual acts of caring and dedication of the EMS first responders at Ground Zero. He also would like to share with them stories of how EMS responders dealt with this horrendous mass casualty incident as well as lessons learned from the catastrophic consequences of that MCI so they may learn from their experience and stay safe in the future.

Contents

INTRODUCTION

September 11, 2001 is a day in American history that has left an indelible memory on all who experienced the aftermath of the terrorist attacks on the World Trade Center in New York. Within the inner circle of New York City Emergency Medical Services (EMS) there are stories told of caring, dedication and sacrifice by EMTs and paramedics at the World Trade Center.

"Everyday Heroes" is a term used to describe EMTs and paramedics who care for patients regardless of race, color, religion or social status and do it without recognition. September 11, 2001 demanded EMTs and paramedics to give their utmost caring, courage and dedication. Some EMS providers also gave their lives during the collapse of the World Trade Center. This book documents the stories of some of the EMTs and paramedics who took the downwind walk to rescue victims of this tragedy. Their spirit represents the best of EMS.

I was a member of the FDNY (Fire Department of New York) EMS in the Bronx who was deployed with the Federal Emergency Management Association (FEMA) at Ground Zero. I feel privileged to have worked with so many EMTs and paramedics who shared with me the details of their experiences on September 11, 2001. I believe my unique role during the tragic events gives me a vantage point from which I can share some of these stories and lessons learned.

I am proud to have worked with several of the EMTs and paramedics who gave the "ultimate sacrifice" or succumbed to exposure in the months following the collapse of the Twin Towers. I feel that since I knew so many of these people, I have a responsibility to share stories not only about their circumstances on 9/11 but also how we knew them in life.

Many EMTs and paramedics are struggling to put these events behind them and forget the tragedy of that ominous September morning. I have looked back on that day to try to reconcile the magnitude of this horrendous tragedy. After mentally reliving the sights, sounds, and smells and sifting through the debris of that September 11th, I feel that caring and courage alone are the only things left intact among the ashes. I think it is important to tell the EMS story so those who want to know how EMS providers dealt with this tragedy can understand the breadth of caring and the depth of our loss.

Because these acts of courage show humanity at its best in the worst moments in the history of our country, they serve as a source of inspiration and hope that shines like a lone ray of light out of the smoke and dust of Ground Zero. Courage in the face of adversity is a source of inspiration for us and, therefore, these stories should be shared. While September 11, 2001 is a unique American tragedy, dealing with devastation is a common theme. I feel that humanity can be strengthened by the examples of the courageous EMS providers who have gone before us.

I am writing this book so future EMTs and paramedics will know the individual acts of caring and dedication of my brothers and sisters in EMS. I would like to share with them stories of how we dealt with this horrendous incident so they may learn from our experience. These "Everyday Heroes" who gave the ultimate sacrifice, survived the collapse of the Twin Towers, or helped with the rescue efforts provided care that was anything but every day routine.

Some EMTs and paramedics who were not at Ground Zero feel they did not make worthwhile contributions. However, the providers who helped by responding to 911 calls or helped fallen coworkers made a significant contribution to patient care and public service.

By sharing these stories of caring and dedication by EMS responders, together we can appreciate the untold acts of selflessness which exemplify the best humanity has to offer in the worst moments of people's lives.

We in EMS want the public to know they we are not icons; we were people with real lives who went to work one day in September. I want these EMTs and paramedics to be remembered as more than faces on a poster, or names read out loud every anniversary of the tragedy. Equally important, I want the EMTs and paramedics who died after September 11th whose names are not read out loud each anniversary to be remembered.

After hearing the stories of those who perished, we realize the seemingly random events that claimed their lives could have also taken our lives. This realization is what makes the events of 9/11 most startling to those who of us who were there.

Chief Daniel Nigro spoke at the EMS memorial service held at Saint Paul's Chapel in May of 2002. I have heard no statement truer than Chief Nigro's concerning the psychological impact of 9/11 when he said, "…this one will be with us the rest of our lives."

Already, there are a large percentage of New York City EMTs and paramedics who were as young as 10 years old during the 9/11 attacks. These EMTs and paramedics were too young to have felt the impact of September 11th, so for them this tragedy is not as vibrant a memory as it is for those of us who served during the event.

People have heard the popular stories of September 11, 2001 that tell of heroism on airline flights, in the Twin Towers and at the Pentagon. I believe it is important for Americans to know of the sacrifice and dedication of EMS responders, as well. Now is the time to share their stories and to teach the lessons learned as the 10th Anniversary of 9/11 looms on the horizon as ominously as the smoke and dust filled the atmosphere after the collapse of the Twin Towers.

Come take the downwind walk with me in my dusty boots as I recount the events, sights, smells, and vivid memories of that unforgettable September, from eye level at Ground Zero.

The World Trade Center Façade in 1989

PART ONE
Life at FDNY EMS
Battalion 55 Before 9/11

I shall pass through this world but once. If therefore there is any kindness I can show or any good deed I can do, let me do it now, for I shall not pass this way again.
— Author Unknown

I

Sweet Summer's End.
Friday September 7, 2001

I slowly climbed the old wrought iron steps to the apparatus floor as I started another day at work. I was always mystified how I do a sixteen-hour tour and then come back the next day at 06:30 hours, on time. I held my cup of tea firmly as I climbed the stairs. The tea gives me the jumpstart I need to get up to operating speed.

I was working at EMS Battalion 55 for the Fire Department of New York (FDNY) Emergency Medical Services (EMS) Command. Holding my tea as I reached the top of the stairs, in front of me I saw a closet that used to house the hay for the horses that pulled the steam fire engines in the early 1900s. The bright morning sun glared in through the security gate enclosed window, warming my face. I was glad this summer was coming to an end because overtime and the summer heat had left me tired. My tea gave me energy and the solitude to prepare for the events of the day.

Our station is referred to as Old Engine 71 in FDNY parlance. This station was built in 1906 and housed Engine 71 for over eighty years. The firehouse was then used to house the Bronx Base of the Fire Marshals and is now shared by the Fire Marshals and EMS. The structure of Battalion 55 is classic red brick and concrete with sculpted concrete details in the front of the building. The history of the FDNY may be lost on many who pass through this building daily, but I appreciate the legacy and history of this building and the FDNY.

As a teenager, I read a book called *Report from Engine Company 82* by Dennis Smith. I was impressed at the seriousness of firefighting and the tenacity of the Bronx. I was proud to be serving with the FDNY in an historic building like this even though my journey into the FDNY was convoluted. I rode in the Bronx in July of 1984 as a paramedic student from the Northeastern University Paramedic Program and started working for New York City Health and Hospital EMS, otherwise known as NYC EMS. Mayor Giuliani merged the NYC EMS with the FDNY on March 17, 1996 to optimize resources and help save response time to rescue patients in cardiac arrest.

As I walked across the apparatus floor, I saw Lieutenant John McBride in the Lieutenants' office. To begin my morning ritual I said, "Good morning John."

"Steve....What the....." John grinned from ear to ear. "You couldn't bring me a coffee?" he said in a patronizing way.

Annoyed due to my tired condition I apologized saying, "John, I'm sorry. I'm so tired today."

John is a redheaded Irish man who loves the fire service. He comes from a family of civil servants and chose to be a paramedic. His father is a police officer and his brother works for sanitation. John volunteers as a firefighter on his days off and works as a paramedic at a local ambulance service on Long Island to maintain his skills. He smiled and opened his arms in a sweeping gesture revealing the red suspenders he likes to wear.

I said, "John, just tell me what is going on?"

He replied, "Steve, you're running one hundred percent of your units today. Nineteen-Charlie is picking up crew at Battalion Fourteen. J.J. is already on patrol dropping overtime personnel back at Battalion 17. I reviewed defibrillator protocols with the EMTs; we checked all the expirations on the defibrillators and the pads. Steve, I'm hurt you didn't bring me coffee."

Only slightly embarrassed, I said, "Stay, John. I'll go pick one up for you after I check the radios and complete the rundown."

He answered, "Nah, I got to run. I'm working on the Island today."

"Take care," I replied as Lt. McBride slips out of the office and down the stairs to his car. I thought it was strange John didn't stay to chat. He likes a joke as much as the next guy, or maybe more, but he also takes time to train the EMTs and medics in patient care and safety. John takes great pride in describing the detail and on the job knowledge about running calls to his employees. John is always saying, "The devil is in the detail, Steve." I thought, "He will probably be in the Haz Tac unit one day."

I started my daily routine by accounting for the radios and equipment, and logging on to the dispatch computer. The computer monitors all the units and assignments in the area we cover, the South Bronx. J.J. was on patrol as Conditions 5-5 and I had "desk duty." A Conditions car is the term used for an EMS lieutenant who responds to help units in the field. We were called "patrol bosses" until we were merged with the fire department.

The vehicle that belongs to our designation is a 1998 Chevrolet Suburban that runs seven days a week, twenty-four hours a day. These vehicles put up with abuse and rough roads that would make a Michigan test track driver run for cover.

We give our in-service signal by logging in using a notebook computer mounted in the truck, which allows us to look up the status of our units, hospitals and call information. When EMS units are dispatched to a job, the call data comes up on their screen. Status signals such as 10-63 responding, 10-88 at scene and 10-82 transporting to the hospital are entered electronically to save radio airtime. We average in excess of 3,000 calls daily over ten radio frequencies. On the busiest days in the high summer heat or a winter blizzard our system sometimes exceeds 4,000 ambulance calls a day.

By using the Mobile Data Terminal (MDT) to transmit "signals" we help free up radio time for radio communications. We are trained to stay off the radio as much as possible to allow the constant radio traffic of assigning jobs and dealing with problems to continue so people needing an ambulance do not have to wait an extraordinarily long time. The saying, "Every second counts" is very true in emergency medicine.

I returned to the office to finish preparing a Tour Three roster of units we were running on a report we call a *Tour Rundown*. FDNY EMS runs three tours a day. Tour One is midnights, Tour Two is days, and Tour Three is the evening shift. Our units are either advanced life support with two paramedics or basic life support with two emergency medical technicians called EMTs.

As I was filling in the Tour Three run down with names and shield numbers of personnel and the status of vehicles assigned to the station, I was interrupted by a Tour One unit member walking into the office who said, "Lou, we need a spare vehicle, our side compartment door doesn't lock."

I stopped what I was doing, grabbed some graphite from the drawer and walked outside to check their vehicle. The door was intact, but the lock mechanism was jammed. A small dose of graphite does not resolve the problem.

I asked the EMT, "How did you go all night with a door that doesn't secure?"

EMT Smith replied while smirking, "L-T, we just noticed it now."

"Yeah, right," I thought.

I looked at them with suspicion. I wondered, "Did they not check their vehicle or did it really just happen now? No matter, we have to get the unit in service."

I told the EMTs, "OK, take vehicle ninety-seven, it's spare, I'll put you off-service." The phone rings and I briskly walked back to the office.

"Good morning Lieutenant, I need your Tour Three Rundown," the RCC (Resource Coordination Center) EMT states curtly.

I nicely reply with "You'll have it in a few minutes. I just walked in the door. Please put 19-Charlie Tour One off-service mechanical, switching into vehicle ninety-seven."

I heard a "Will do!" and then a click, as the EMT at RCC abruptly hung up the phone. "Nice day to you too!" I thought. I returned to finishing the rundown.

Then I remembered my cup of tea. I wondered, "Where *is* my tea? Did I leave it in the locker room?" I walked over the apparatus floor to my locker; no tea on top. Did I leave it in my car, *no*. I walked in with it. Where could it be?" The phone rang.

I jogged back to the office; I answered the phone "Good morning, Lieutenant Kanarian, Battalion 55."

On the other end I heard, "Stevie, my lad, how many times must I tell you, I take my tea, milk with no sugar!"

"John!" I thought. "John, don't mess with my tea, I'm serious."

"Ha, Ha, Ha," John chuckled to me on the phone. "Oh by the way, I hope you have a *Quiet* day. I had a big breakfast and now I am going to bed."

"Damn that guy, I thought." John chuckled again as he hung up.

Humor and good-natured joking around are part of the EMS culture. EMS providers have a dark-sided sense of humor we call *gallows humor*, which is not understood by the average person. This offbeat sense of humor is a way for us to balance the stress of the job and to deal in some way with the death and dying we see. It is also a way of sharing the brotherhood of our job.

However, Joking around for John is much deeper. It is a way of life for him to joke around and "get you" when he can.

"That's ok; I'll get him down the road," I thought, smiling about the possible options I have to make a strong comeback.

Mike Condon arrived in my office and greeted me with, "Good Morning, Steve."

"Hi Mike, how are you?"

"Margaret here yet?" he asked as he looked over the rundown and what to expect for the day.

"Not yet." I replied.

Mike is an experienced EMT with more than fifteen years experience. We call Mike the "Mayor" of Hunts Point because he has been on the same unit for so long that he knows all the cops, the business owners and the homeless people in Hunts Point. A warm "What's wrong, Ma?" from Mike puts most patients at ease.

Mike had first name status with me because of his experience. Most guys call you *boss* or *Lou*, short for Lieutenant, but for guys like Mike — whom I have broken ribs with during CPR (cardiopulmonary resuscitation), backed up, and lifted patients with for many years — the respect runs deep.

His partner, Margaret, is also an experienced EMT who is glad to be on a slower unit in Hunts Point with a partner who does not attract attention. Margaret is a single mom raising a teen. She makes super "gravy," which is what true Italians call sauce, I am told. The best of all things with Mike is that he and I can disagree and yell one day and the next day he greets you with the same "G'mornin, Bossman." Mike sees the big picture and does not easily get stressed. He helps me keep an even keel — kind of like a buoy on stormy seas.

With the stress involved working EMS in the Bronx, co-workers often find fault with each other or bump heads on issues and build resentment. But, we have a true, mature relationship. We like to work as a team, but in reality the challenges of dealing with the stress and unrelenting nature of the job sometimes drives us apart. However, when the chips are down, everybody works together to get the job done. My job as a lieutenant was to realize the issues people have and to know how best to get them to do their work and balance their needs as well as the needs of the patients they serve.

Mike continued on with his greeting, "Good morning my brother, how are you today? Stressing already with Tour One BS?"

I said, "John took my tea."

Mike laughs and said, "Ohh, no, not your tea! Mel-low my brother, mel-low," as he effortlessly breezed out of the office.

It's amazing how such a big guy can move so quietly. Mike is about six foot three and naturally very strong. He speaks with an accent even though he is from New York City. I think the accent is just his way of dealing with stress and focusing it back into the world where it came from. Some employees require a lot of attention; others, like Mike, do what they are supposed to do and require very little maintenance. Mike is a pleasure to have in my station. Mike logs on to the MDT, gives his in-service signal and disappears into the streets.

Units in our system are deployed to Cross Street Locations (CSL) to ensure a quicker response time. With over seventy ambulances in the Bronx this system of posting units on street corners expedites response times. However, it is not the most comfortable experience when you have to sit on a street corner for sixteen hours.

I had one hour until the next unit arrived for tour change. I completed the rundown putting down personnel names and shield numbers, vehicle numbers, listing who was out sick and what vehicles were out for repair, then faxed the rundown to RCC and stapled the confirmation sheet to the rundown. Next, I walked out to the apparatus floor and looked around the garage. More often than not, I loaded the supplies into the rack on the apparatus floor then swept the floor. I like a well-stocked and clean station. This is probably a throwback to working in my uncle's grocery store as a teen where I maintained the supplies in the basement and kept the shelves stocked. I also worked as the paramedic coordinator in Queens where I kept the medic room stocked and checked the spare medic equipment. I liked to have the shelves stocked and the station swept so people coming to work get a good start.

I saw an ambulance pull up in front of the station and start to back in. The sun was bright and warm as the light reflected off the ambulance's trademark red, yellow and white FDNY colors. I thought, "What a beautiful day. Soon autumn will bring the cool weather and temperatures will not be so hot all day."

EMT Buccieri, who we call "Booch," walked in uttering "Hi boss. I need some defib (defibrillator) pads, lost another one."

"How old?" I inquired.

He answered, "Seventy-nine year old woman."

"Practice makes perfect Booch," I replied, trying to make light of a bad situation and continued with "Good morning Booch."

"If it is I hadn't noticed." He grunted. I asked Booch what was bothering him. He replies with "Oh, late night with the boys is all." Booch turned his head a little and continued, "Actually I wish I had worked out more for that fire physical. I would be graduating from the Fire Academy today."

Booch was from a family of firefighters. His father and step-father were both FDNY Lieutenants. He had grown up hanging out at firehouses with his dad. Unfortunately, he had not scored a 100% on the firefighter physical. It seemed like Booch knew most of the older firemen on the job in the South Bronx. He is a young guy who will probably be better prepared for the physical test next time. He continued lamenting, "If I had done better on that physical I would be graduating this week and working a *real* job."

I asked, "You don't think that woman in arrest thought what happened was real? Was she alone?"

9

He grunts, "No, she had her husband there."

"Geez, Booch, for the husband that is as real as it gets. How long where they married for? Thirty or forty years?"

Booch answered, "I don't know boss. I've stopped asking."

"Hell, I know. I'm just bummed she died and wish the City paid us more."

I tried to console him by remarking, "I know. Better luck with the FDNY physical next time Booch."

I sat down at the desk and pulled the office chair in close. I thought, "Time to update the log and complete some of the daily paperwork, then get some quiet time for some tea, and watch ESPN to see how the Jets and Giants are doing." My quiet time was interrupted with a Beep, beep, beep. Damn, that was a quick ten minutes. What now, I wondered. I saw vehicle 399 backing into the garage. I thought, "Mike and Margaret are back? What could be wrong? They just left the station." Mike eases out of the ambulance giving his knees a chance to adjust, then settling into his usual limp.

"Stevie, here is a hot tea, large, milk and sugar, just the way you like it. Enjoy, Boss Man."

I'm touched by his thoughtfulness. I let loose a great big grin of happiness knowing I have the respect of my coworkers and together we get through the day. I turned to Mike and said, "Thank you, Mike. Thank you very much."

"We have to look out for each other, Boss Man." Mike replied, as he walked back to the ambulance.

"Yes we do Mike, have a great day!"

I went into the office and sat back in my chair. A good boss knows the strength and weaknesses of each employee. A good EMT always knows what a partner or his boss needs to get on an even keel; it is a relationship much like a marriage. I opened my tea and updated the Station logbook. Sipping my hot tea, I felt at peace.

I saw the *New York Times* and thought "John must have left it here." I thumbed through the pages looking at the headlines. "Funny how John has time to read the paper and all his Tour One units come in needing things on Tour 2. Hmm...Coincidence? Do his units plain need things and he farms them off on Tour 2 or is Tour 1 that unlucky? I wondered.

EMT Sanchez from 0-3-King Tour 1 returned to the office to turn in his radio and keys. He said, "Boss can we get four Proventils and another book of ACRs?" (Ambulance Call Reports).

"What the hell, don't you guys do anything on Tour 1?" I asked.

"Lt. McBride said to come back after 06:30 because he was busy," Charlie said trying to hold in a smile.

"John!" I cursed to myself.

I thought to myself, "I like a joke, but not just before my cup of morning tea. Because of John, I am still working on my first cup of tea."

Charlie confessed, "John knew you would be tired and wanted to mess with you." Laughing he walks out of the office. I gritted my teeth and thought, "I'll get that joker good."

Now, time to return the favor to John. I called the dispatch center for the ambulance service John works for and said, "Hi! This is Lieutenant Kanarian."

"Lieutenant, nice to hear your voice, this is Lisa. How have you been? What can I do for you?"

I said, "John McBride is working Medic 3 and he is very upset."

Lisa asked, "Why L-T?"

I continued, "John has a hot medic student he wants to impress but he does not have any jobs. He was wondering if you could send him on all the nursing home runs so his student can get some tubes."

Lisa said, "No problem L-T. I thought he liked it slow. I will move him up to first out."

I added, "Thank you Lisa, you're the best."

She followed with a sweet sounding, "Bye L-T."

I thought, "Ha, ha, ha, John you are so screwed. Instead of sleeping all day he can work his ass off like the rest of the world."

Pete, one of the paramedics, walked into the office; he wanted to show me something interesting to tell my students. Since he knew I teach for the Paramedic Program at a local community college, he wanted to tell me about a patient he had in ventricular tachycardia.

Pete explained, "The patient was stable at first and did not respond to Lidocaine. We gave him the 1.5 milligrams per kilo of Lidocaine and nothing changed. Then we gave the drip. When he developed chest pain we called to sedate him with Valium and cardiovert him. He converted to a junctional rhythm and then sinus. Wildest thing Steve, we get to the ED (emergency department) and the guy goes back into VTach (ventricular tachycardia) again. Synchronized cardioversion didn't work. So, the doc gives him 2 grams of mag (magnesium sulfate) and he converts like a charm. I asked the doc, Why the mag? The doc told me he has seen VTach convert with magnesium sulfate on several occasions because many patients are dehydrated and depleted of mag sulfate."

"Impressive," I remarked. I told Pete "I appreciate the thought," and praised him on a job well done. I asked, "Can I keep these strips?"

"Sure boss," he replied.

Pete is an experienced medic who takes pride in patient care and lets the organizational crap run off his shoulders; he is a real professional who exhibits a "positive stethoscope sign." The stethoscope sign is what I call it when a provider wears his stethoscope around his neck, which indicates to me he cares about patient care. If an EMT wears a bulletproof vest and sunglasses it tells me he is more interested in being a cop, not a medic. There are people who are more into how they look, their hair, and their car. This tells me they care more about themselves than anything else. I like to see the positive stethoscope sign. Patient care is what we are here for. I like this!

I like to read people by what they are wearing, what they represent, the tell tale signs they exhibit. For instance a police officer takes pride in having a baton that is worn and having the leather strap a certain length so he can twirl the baton while standing in the street.

A firefighter tells you he is experienced by the wear and tear on his turnout coat. Older firemen have been in so many fires they have slightly melted helmets. A firefighter is known by the tool he carries. The entry guy has the irons. The OV (overhead ventilation) guy carries the ax and goes over the fire to vent the roof. These are the signs that tell others, "I have been around. I know my shit."

Pete is known as a medic who cares about his patients because he does his best for his patients and wears a stethoscope around his neck. That is how I see things.

The phone rang, and my spare moment was interrupted again. I picked up the phone and it was Captain Laurie Santo. Laurie Santo was a widely respected captain who started the Quality Assurance and Improvement (QA/I) unit twelve years ago and was recently promoted to Captain. She started the call with "Good morning Steve, it's Laurie. How are things at the station today?"

I replied "Good Captain. Hectic, but good."

Laurie continued, "I'm sorry, I'm downtown again and I'm training someone to take over my job."

I replied, "Laurie we know you're there temporarily until you get called back to headquarters. They do that with all the rising stars."

"Steve, I'll be there and part of the time at the station, it just takes time," she told me.

I answered, "That would be great to have you here."

Laurie Santo is an understanding and intelligent person who sees the potential in each of us. As head of the QA/I unit, she is respected and consulted with by Chiefs of the respective boroughs. Laurie is top notch in my book for both her people skills and for being one of the folks who shaped our system. She was assigned to Battalion 55 after she was promoted. We are a small station in the South Bronx, which runs seven units. The Battalion and the officers here have a reputation of taking care of business on our own. So, I was guessing she was here temporarily before being moved back to headquarters. I thought, "If Captain Santo says she is really coming here, I guess it will be so."

"Was that Laurie?" asked Rick, another one of the EMTs at Battalion 55, as he strode into the office.

I replied, "Yes, she was checking in."

Rick came into the office with a drill and toolbox and had the wind at his back. He said, "Laurie wants me to hang these photos today and put her files in the cabinet."

"Hmm, maybe she will be here full time," I thought.

Rick is a real asset to the station. He had over twelve years in the streets and is an excellent EMT who knows how to handle all situations and negotiate with the cops and bosses in the field. He is a great help in the station, and we need more EMTs like him on the street. He is on light duty for a knee injury and may require surgery.

My attention quickly turned to the radio when I heard the number 10-13, which is the code for officer needs assistance. The dispatcher repeated, "The address is 1510 Grand Concourse, the time is 10:13 hours." The first time I had only heard the number 10-13 not the job that went along with the time. Some numbers trigger a different response. 10-13 is one of those numbers because it is associated with an emergency where a police officer needs assistance. Fortunately it was only the time, not an actual emergency. This type of startle response is called a "trigger" which reminds a person of some traumatic or stressful event in their lives.

I spent the remainder of the day updating attendance calendar cards, employee time sheets, placing the medical supply order, and dealing with any questions and issues that surfaced. Oscar, one of the Fire Marshals upstairs came in with his cup of coffee and we talked about our jobs and how they contrasted. Oscar complained about the lack of overtime and the fact that their contract has been overdue for two years. I guessed there were common issues despite our different jobs.

Before I knew it, the time was 1:45 p.m., almost time to go home. I went to the front of the station and enjoyed the hot bright sun, which was unusual for September. I admired the ninety-plus year old firehouse our station was located in and admired the intricate concrete shapes over the main entrance. I thought, "They don't make buildings like this anymore! What a cool job to have and to be part of the FDNY history." I heard a horn blow across the street. I looked over and saw people arguing over a parking spot in front of the 25-story high rise that loomed over our station, which is located opposite several high-rise public housing projects. I thought it was cool; there was less distance to travel when they called the ambulance.

Our Conditions vehicle, a 1998 Suburban, returned to the station with Lieutenant Scotch on board.

I asked, "How are you?"

He replied "Good, Steve, even better when I get home."

"I hear that." I replied.

Steve and Neil pulled their ambulance into the garage bay to decontaminate after a job. "What did you guys have?" I asked.

"We had a bad ped (pedestrian) struck. A girl was hit while

14

crossing the concourse. Fourteen years old, she didn't even know what hit her. Fractured pelvis, bilateral femurs and a fractured skull." Neil, looked away while spraying the floor with water, clots of blood flow from the ambulance into the drain. He continued, "Worst thing was, she was holding her sister's hand; the other girl was fine."

Neil asked, "Why do the most messed up jobs happen on the nicest days? I don't know Steve, but it sure is the truth."

I agreed.

My relief came in for Tour 3. The Tour 3 Lieutenant greeted me saying "Good afternoon Steve. What's going on?"

I told him, "You have 100% of your units today, 2 sick calls which were covered with overtime and vehicle 1024 went out of service mechanical. Have a good night. See you tomorrow."

As I walked toward my locker, the Tour 3 personnel were getting their equipment together, polishing their shoes and chatting about everyday things. The Tour 3 Lieutenant bellows, "C'mon, boys and girls, log on, and get in service. It's hot and busy!" I am always amazed at the tenacity of New York City and the relentless job at hand for EMS.

I changed my sweaty shirt and put on a dry t-shirt. I gathered my equipment and headed down to my car. I looked forward to the drive home and a chance to relax.

II
"Signal 10-40, Plane Crash."
Saturday September 8, 2001

T he drive into work, down the Palisades Parkway, was a beautiful trip on a Saturday morning. The commuters were all off the road for the weekend and I enjoyed driving down the Parkway to work. As I drove, I thought, "Today is especially beautiful. I can see the blue sky over the trees and the bright sun is warming my face. The bright green colors of the trees and the morning sun are inspiring. This is going to be a great day!"

I slowed down to pay the George Washington Bridge toll. I crossed over the bridge and into Manhattan exiting off the Deegan Expressway in the Bronx. My commute took me by Yankee Stadium every day. Passing by the Stadium, then under the elevated train on River Avenue, the contrast was stark. Millionaires play baseball games in a park in an area where people were just barely making it.

I saw partiers from the night before leaving the diner and slowly walking up the sidewalk to hail a cab. I saw a drunken woman and man trying to prop each other up. She was wearing black nylons with a diamond pattern in the back and a dress that was too short and too small for her size. He was wearing a white suit with a salmon shirt and a large white fedora with a red feather. "Damn, they are drunk but having fun together and enjoying life," I thought.

I arrived at work and had my tea firmly in hand. I strolled into the office with my tea and a coffee for John. I greeted Lt. McBride with a cheerful "Good Morning."

He replied, "Oh, you got some sleep last night uh, Stevie."

I answered, "Yes, I did." I held on to my tea tightly as I watched him. He smiled; he was not getting one over on me today. I am feeling great. "And how was your day?" I asked.

He replied, "Why do you ask? I got screwed as a matter of fact. I did more jobs yesterday than in the previous four shifts."

I remarked, "I guess you should not mess with me when I am your dispatcher's favorite lieutenant when she used to work at 26 as a rookie." I grinned from ear to ear, swirling my cup so the water gets all of the tea flavor from the bag.

John exclaimed, "Damn, that was you? They had me running from one end of Long Island to another."

"Yup, I told Lisa you had a medic student." I chuckled, "Sweet revenge."

"I have a surprise for you today, Steve," John tells me with a smile.

I hesitated. Then he continued, "You're going to the Operation Low Key, the drill at LaGuardia Airport today."

I responded with, "Yeah, right, big joke."

He replied, "No joke, you're going."

"Cool!" I thought, "Awesome!"

Operation Low Key is a yearly drill to assess emergency preparedness response to aviation accidents at LaGuardia. A 10-40 is a confirmed plane crash. I have never been to one. One day I will get to one I'm sure. I have had run of the mill jobs as opposed to people who are always running into crazy calls. I looked forward to the drill.

Lt. McBride told me "Helio is in; he has the desk today." This was good news for me. Heliodoro Mendes and I have worked on and off together for about ten years.

I thought, "What a great day to be on patrol. It will nice to be challenged rather than have the same monotony."

Being on patrol as an EMS supervisor is a mixed bag of fun and responsibility. On the one hand, you can set your own agenda for the day as long as you stay within the margins of what the chiefs want you to do. The day consists of clearing the emergency room of units when they back up, dealing with mechanical issues of ambulances and mitigating problems EMS providers run into. We respond to refusals of medical assistance (RMA) calls to assist the crews in convincing the patient to go to the hospital. People often are apprehensive about ambulance transport even when they are in need of care. We also get to respond to jobs and assist with patient care. Some units appreciate the help and experience a boss brings.

EMS supervisors also coordinate patient care at mass casualty incidents (MCIs). We coordinate patient care, triage, and act as command of EMS resources on the scene. We work under the direction of the fire chief when we are at a fire.

I continued on with my day by driving over to the Emergency Room at Bronx Lebanon Hospital and speaking with the unit going to the drill. I wanted to make sure they had their safety coats, helmets and a supply of triage tags. I also reviewed the procedure for the use of triage tags with the crew because most EMTs and medics often forget how to do triage because the skill is not used often. We talked about the drill and what to expect, and above all how not to attract attention. I wished them well and returned to my command car.

The Chevrolet Suburbans that we drive on patrol is loaded with first aid supplies, a semi-automatic defibrillator and spare long boards in case of an MCI. The day was warm, sunny and pleasant. Sitting in my vehicle and enjoying the weather I heard the AM radio DJ report about the Yankees and Red Sox playing in the Bronx that day. The Red Sox coming to town was always a big rivalry. Since it was early in the afternoon, I saw the tour buses and crowds grow.

"2–6 Frank, 2–6 William cardiac arrest," the dispatcher voice cuts through the radio waves. "Need 2–6 Frank and 2–6 William for a cardiac arrest 156 and Webster Avenue.

The Unit answered, "Frankie, got it."

26 William responded, "William, send it over."

I said, "Conditions 5–5 send it also."

"You got it, Conditions," the dispatcher replied.

The assignment text came over the MDT, "CARDIAC ARREST. Caller states 6-month old baby blue and not breathing, caller starting chest compressions." The hair stood up on my head and neck. I reached down and turned on the emergency lights and my foot pressed the accelerator down all in one combined motion. I passed through traffic and stopped at the red light, accelerated, and then proceeded straight down Webster, watching for pedestrians, and cars making u-turns.

I saw the units on the scene. I heard over the radio, "26 Zebra, have the BLS (basic life support) set up in the bus, we are coming down, CPR in progress."

I pulled up in front of the scene and saw the engine company parked in front of the building. The chauffeur yelled out, "They're pumping and blowing boss."

I waved and said "Thanks."

He continued, "They are bringing the kid down."

A group of rescuers were huddled together holding a tiny 6-month old infant on a shirt backboard. One firefighter was doing CPR, another was holding the IV and monitor, while the medic was ventilating the child, maintaining a good chin tilt and ensuring chest rise. We placed the child in the back of the bus and went to work.

"I got the IV (intravenous drip)," the medic said.

His partner called, "I got airway."

I stated, "I'll draw up the meds."

The EMT told me, "Boss we met them in the hallway. The child was found cold and unresponsive. She slept in bed with the parents." We looked at each other realizing putting the child in a crib may have prevented this death.

Partner states, "Asystole."

Asystole is a complete lack of cardiac activity and has a very poor outcome for survival. Collectively we know the infant has been pulseless for too long. We pushed Epinephrine, Atropine and Dextrose, continued CPR and started rolling to the hospital. The EMT and the medic monitored the child as we provided compressions and ventilations, trying to pump life into this vacant little body. As we approached the hospital we could see some nurses who have come out to greet the patient. We told them that the patient is 6 months old, unknown downtime, and slept with parents.

I said, "We've given Epinephrine three times. There's been no change."

The mass of people went up to the ED with the lifeless child. The job went well but the outcome had already been determined. I went into the ED and washed my hands. Pandemonium erupted in the ED as the mother arrived screaming "MYYY baa-by!"

"Time to go," I thought.

The fire department may not like the merger with EMS and the runs they now have to do on top of the fires, but it is nice to have hands-on-chest quickly in an arrest situation. Despite our differences, NYPD (New York Police Deparmtent), FDNY (Fire Department of New York) and EMS (Emergency Medical Services) all come together when a child's life is in the balance. It is a great feeling to be part of such a team when things are going well.

I started the Suburban and put on my seatbelt. I pushed the 10–98 button indicating I was available.

The dispatcher retorted back "Conditions 5–5, Conditions 5–5 switch to citywide for the drill."

I acknowledged the dispatcher, "Conditions 5–5, 10–4."

It's time to go, I put the truck in gear and drove the Grand Concourse and entered the Bruckner Boulevard to go to Queens. For months at a time we stay in our borough and never leave to go to Manhattan or Queens. "This is nice!" I thought. "I am going to LaGuardia Airport for the day."

Crossing the Triboro Bridge I saw New York City and the East River. Being born in Massachusetts, I am always cognizant of the beauty of this city. EMS professionals understand how frail life can be and we enjoy moments like this.

The emergency plan for LaGuardia Airport has designated a pre-planned staging area. Knowing the plan I drove to the staging and waited for instructions. Staging is organized by agency: FDNY, NYC EMS, NYPD right on down the line. I guessed they never got around to removing the NYC EMS signs when we merged with the New York City Fire Department in 1996. Entrance and exit to the runway is severely limited to a vehicle escorted by the Port Authority Police.

A message popped up on the computer, "All units responding to operation Low Key report to building thirty-four for the drill briefing."

I drove to building thirty-four and entered the briefing room. It was always nice to see lieutenants, EMTs and medics from other parts of the city. We each operate in our respective boroughs and give little thought the other parts of the city. It is somewhat daunting to think of the size of New York, the area and number of people we cover.

"Good morning ladies and gentleman," Chief McCracken's voice boomed out.

Chief McCracken is the Chief in Charge of EMS operations, second in Command. He is a large Irishman whose very size requires you to look up to him. The chief continued, "Today is an important drill for preparation for an aviation accident or a MCI. I know you all will do a good job."

A captain met with the lieutenants assigned to the drill and asked us which role we wanted in the incident command structure for EMS operations. He said, "I need a communications liaison, triage officer, tracking officer, transport officer and a safety officer."

I heard one lieutenant say, "I'll take staging." Another said, "I will take treatment." Someone took tracking. I spoke up, "I will take triage."

I got a shoulder from the lieutenant next to me. He said, "Triage is chaos, don't take that one, trust me."

I looked at him and smiled, "I know. I want to give it a try."

"Kanarian, you got triage," the captain bellowed.

For many years I have been an instructor who teaches MCI operations and learning from my mistakes in the field. I felt I had to give triage a run for my money to let me prove what I teach. I also worked in Queens as ALS (advanced life support) Coordinator and attended planning meetings for the airport. I honestly wanted to do the difficult job of triage and see how I did.

The drill commenced.

We staged in the pre-planned staging location and awaited the start of the drill. While I was waiting I mentally reviewed START, which stands for simple treatment and rapid triage. We were only supposed to treat life threatening injuries that can easily be corrected, triage the patient immediately as delayed, ambulatory or deceased, and then move on to triage the next patient.

A crucial point that EMTs and paramedics have not been trained adequately to understand is in an MCI we are only supposed to treat the patients that are most likely to *survive*. Typically in daily EMS operations we treat the most critically injured patients first. In an MCI if we expend personnel on a mortal wound we will lose several other patients that can be saved.

My thought was interrupted as an announcement was made. "Beee-eeep. Attention all Citywide units a signal 10–40 is reported at LaGuardia Airport, this is a drill, this is a drill, this is a drill."

The announcement sent personnel into a business-like series of brisk movements. We all put our coat on, helmet on, and buttoned up, fixed the radio on the outside of the coat. Let's go. The first wave of emergency vehicles is escorted by the PAPD (Port Authority Police Department). The PAPD escorts vehicles on and off the runway; nobody drives on the Tarmac without an escort. The PAPD officers are in contact with the control tower.

As we turned the bend onto the runway I could see the plane with patients strewn around the runway, and to the left a fire was burning to simulate a burning aircraft. A lime green fire truck bolted from my right and speeded by. In one coordinated move the turret on the front of the truck turned on and swept forward to the fire and a stream of water sprayed from the turret nozzle an impressive 200 feet away. In a few seconds the thick acrid black smoke turned to white steam. I thought, "That was very cool. The fire was knocked down."

A signal 10–40 is a confirmed plane crash. A signal 10–39 is a standby at an airport for a plane emergency. A plane emergency can be anything from the plane being low on fuel to an indicator light flashing. A 10–39 is usually a pretty mundane assignment. However, the potential for disaster is always there. The hard part of emergency work is to maintain a readiness and not become jaded by the mundane everyday jobs or the jobs that turn out to be nothing.

The escort stopped on the Tarmac and we set up EMS operations. Radio traffic began. "Operation Low Key Command we are located on runway three zero we have approximately 150 patients."

On the radio I said, "Requesting 10 ALS and 30 BLS units, have units respond to the staging area."

"10–4, K 10 ALS and 30 BLS," the Citywide Dispatch acknowledged.

The Citywide Dispatcher is responsible for handling mass casualty incidents and citywide issues like special events and ambulance accidents. This type of incident interrupts the flow of emergency jobs when held on the regular borough radio frequency. They tend to put the more experienced, calmer dispatchers on the Citywide Dispatch frequency.

I started to focus on the job of triage. I asked myself. "Is the scene safe?" I am on a runway with a plane down, what are the immediate hazards, light smoke, no jet fuel, and no other hazards.

I directed the units with me to start triage and said, "Remember a Red Tag is a patient with resps (respirations) over 30 or less than 8, or absent radial pulses; Green Tag is everybody who can walk and Yellow Tags are the ones left over. Let's go triage all the patients."

I walked among the providers, making sure everyone had their gloves and eye protection on. Firemen were beginning to arrive to help with movement of the patients. I saw a fireman moving a patient and directed him to "put her down, she is a Yellow Tag, Red Tags are immediate life threats, get the red out brother!"

I turned to another fireman and said, "get the red out brother, they are dying!" I gave him a pat on the back to complement his effort and show some team camaraderie.

Next I heard firemen telling other firemen, "Red first, get the red out!"

That was a critical point; we needed Red tags carried to treatment to save lives. Later the Yellow tags would be carried to treatment, and then the Green Tag patients would be escorted to a city bus.

Treatment was surprised that only red tags are coming in and remarked, "What the hell?"

The problem was we do not practice triage enough. The average responder probably responds to two or three MCI's a year. We moved to triage the red tags by priority, airway, the breathing problems, then bleeding, fractures and burns, right down the line. I looked back to the Tarmac and the triage area was littered with paper, blue gloves and a few remaining patients. The last patients were removed in 23 minutes. "Not bad," I thought.

The chatter on the radio continued. I was directed to help in transport; my sector had been shut down. I helped direct the safe loading and proper distribution of patients and the MCI rapidly tailed away. The treatment area was reserved for shipping out patients as quickly as possible and getting the MCI moved off the Tarmac. I headed to the RAC truck to get some Gatorade and dry my face. The soot from the fire and the heat had made me look disheveled; the feel of cool water and some liquid rejuvenated me. I washed my face and the warm sun quickly dried it.

We assembled in the PAPD building to talk about the day's events. Comments were made about not enough information, people not wearing their safety coats, and not enough supplies. The chief gave a review, there was good communication, and this was like a real MCI. He said, "We will go over the results during the post incident critique, which will be scheduled next week." We were all thanked for all our help and complemented on a job well done.

As I walk out I greeted Chief McCracken, "Hi Chief. How did we do?"

He replied, "We'll talk about it at the review."

"How did triage go? Were you pleased we got the red tags out first?"

Again, he told me, "We will talk about it at the review."

"Damn!" I thought. "I did a great job. Probably caught him off guard the way I handled triage. Oh well. I think I did great. We got the patients triaged, got the red out and stayed safe."

Returning to the Bronx in my command car, I drove over the Triboro Bridge and looked at the City skyline on my left. I could see boats in the East River, the United Nations building was in view, and the City was aglow with recreation and optimism. On AM radio I heard the talk about the Emmy Awards and how what dress an actress will be wearing was the big scandal of the week. Venus and Serena were playing tennis in Flushing for the US Open. The Boston Red Sox were playing the Yankees in the Bronx that night. "A great weekend in a great city," I thought.

The warm late summer's air blew in my window as I crossed the bridge into the Bronx. I enjoyed the feeling of a job well done and a day well spent as drove. I thought, "We are off to a great new millennium." I felt the warm sun on my face as I drove back into the Bronx. Then I began to think of that lifeless infant we took to the hospital that morning.

Life is fragile! This is the lesson EMS paramedics and EMTs know all too well. Very fragile indeed!

PART TWO
Terrorist Attacks on the World Trade Center

We will not tire, we will not falter,
and we will not fail.
— President George W. Bush,
Speech after 9/11 attacks

III
Blue Skies Overhead.
Tuesday September 11, 2001

8:57 A.M. Signal 10–40...Number One
World Trade Center

"Beeeeeep. Attention all Bronx units the signal 10–40 has been announced in the borough of Manhattan at Number One World Trade Center. The time is 08:57 hours, and I am dispatcher 2289."

The MCI announcement interrupted my attention to station issues and paperwork. The typical reaction when we hear an announcement of an MCI is, "Well it must be bullshit." EMS personnel are pretty jaded and usually downplay things, by saying things to themselves, like, "This can't be for real" or "This job is not that bad."

I did not think this plane crash job was real. I thought, "The Twin Towers are so big how can someone not see them?" I did not think of terrorism. I simply did not believe it was a real job.

Units were volunteering to respond to the World Trade Center and the Bronx dispatcher advised, "We have enough units please stay available in your area." By nature emergency responders are drawn to the big job to make a difference and do something exciting. Many of the daily jobs become routine to the experienced EMS provider. It may seem weird to become used to someone's cardiac arrest or heart attack but we build up a tolerance to the regular calls. A big job helps break the monotony and challenges EMTs and paramedics to deliver patient care under different circumstances.

Accountability is a big concept of MCI management in EMS, so we discourage freelancing and insist only unit's assigned respond to an MCI. Occasionally units will be nearby and are "flagged down" by a bystander or police officer on the scene.

I looked up the job text in the computer. "Caller states airplane has crashed into the World Trade Center Tower." I looked at the unit status board of the computer and saw there were over twenty units assigned to the call.

I went back to performing my day-to-day ritual of getting units in service, administrative procedures and phone calls. An EMT came in and turned on the TV. I looked up and saw the World Trade Center with smoke pouring out of the Tower.

Some more EMTs come into the office and exclaimed, "They attacked the Pentagon also!"

"What?" I asked.

One EMT responded, "We are under attack boss. Planes have hit the Trade Center and the Pentagon."

I was amazed to see the silhouette of a plane on the side of the Tower, a big plane. This was no touring plane gone awry; this was a jet! "Holy shit!" I thought. "They will be talking about this for years, just like the plane that hit the Empire State Building." I wondered, how they will get the wreckage down from way up there; the Trade Center is much taller than the Empire State Building.

Prior plane accidents in Manhattan included one on July 28, 1945 when a B–25 Bomber hit the Empire State Building due to low visibility. The bomber was being diverted from LaGuardia Airport to Newark Airport when it stuck the 79th floor of the Empire State building causing an explosion. The bomber was subsequently brought down piece by piece to repair the building.

New York City had braced for a terror attack during the New Years' Day celebration for the turn of the century. We had also escaped any glitches with the Y2K threat of computers crashing in the year 2000, and we were sailing through a very peaceful year.

Firefighters and EMS personnel always make comparison to

previous historic incidents. When I first started in EMS, my lieutenant would talk about the JFK plane crash in the 1970s. That was a job others were measured by for years. I responded to the scene of the 1993 bombing of the World Trade Center as a member of FEMA USAR. The Happy Land fire on Southern Boulevard in the Bronx was the largest homicide in United States history at that time. I responded to the Happy Land fire with Paramedic Helene Shanes, the first female paramedic in New York City EMS. The Happy Land fire claimed the lives of 87 people. In my opinion, the 1993 bombing of the World Trade Center didn't eclipse the Happy Land Fire.

I thought, "Firemen are going downtown thinking this is the big job of the new millennium. Funny, again I was not responding. Here I was on desk duty at Battalion 55."

On September 20, 1989 when Flight 5050 crashed in Flushing Bay, I was working in Riverdale, the Bronx. My partner and I tried to volunteer for the call. We radioed in to dispatch, "Central 25 X-Ray we are only 10 minutes out of LaGuardia, send us the 10–40."

"25 X, you want a job?"

"Yes, send it over."

"OK medic, 197 and Creston Avenue, thirty-eight year old difficulty in breathing. Are you 10–63? En route?"

"Bastard," I exclaim. "Next time I am going."

"That isn't right" my partner exhaled shaking his head. We both knew it would be bedlam if everybody showed up. We have to show some discipline, our day will come for the big one.

When flight 405 crashed on March 22, 1992 I was off-duty. Now another plane crash and I am on desk duty. I am pretty much a "white cloud" which is a paramedic who has easy days and always seems to miss the big jobs. A "black cloud" is a person who is always in the middle of the storm. For example a "black cloud" medic goes to a house for difficulty breathing and the building turns out to be on fire, or a shooting erupts while they are carrying the patient down the stairs. I think a lot of luck is how you conduct yourself in the street. You can focus on your patient or you can try to save the world.

"RRRRRooar BAAAAM!" The quick roar of a jet engine was followed by an explosion as the second airliner struck the World Trade Center.

Alexis yelled out, "Oh man! Did you see that? This is unbelievable!"

I began to wonder, "Is this real or is this a media event like war of the worlds?" The thought that we were under attack and airliners were crashing down around the country was unimaginable. I felt the goose bumps on my arms as the hair stood straight up.

The announcer proclaimed, "A second jet has struck the World Trade Center at 9:06 eastern time."

I called the RCC at 9 Metro Tech Plaza and was advised we are under normal operations, no reason to do anything differently; units downtown are handling the job fine.

Lt. Periu called the station and asked, "What is going on Steve? Are they recalling people yet?"

I answered, "No, Felipe not yet; everything is normal operations so far."

On the Bronx radio frequency I heard the dispatcher call units, "2–6 Boy, 1–8 Charlie, 1–5 George…switch to Citywide you are going to the MCI 10–40 in the Borough of Manhattan."

I then heard 18 Charlie advise the dispatcher they had delivered their patient to the hospital and were available to go downtown. "10–4 1–8 Charlie, take it into the 10–40 at 1 World Trade Center. I heard Joe Conzo give the 10–63 and remembered the dispatcher's words, "10–40 at 1 World Trade Center."

Uptown at St. Barnabas Hospital

EMT Yamel Marino left St. Barnabas Hospital and turned to EMT Joe Conzo and said, "See you Joe; we are going to the Trade Center. BLS unit 18 Charlie, EMT Joe Conzo and his partner Billy rushed into the hospital to drop off their patient and respond to the Trade Center. They were anxious to drop off their patient and head downtown to the big job of the new millennium.

Eighteen Charlie accelerated and headed toward the Cross Bronx Expressway. The Westside Highway traffic was backed up because the entrance to Manhattan had been blocked, so 18 Charlie slowly wormed through traffic as cars tried to yield right of way so the ambulance could make it to the World Trade Center. All of a sudden,

18 Charlie contacted another vehicle while squeezing through traffic. Joe and Billy stopped to exchange information.

The driver exclaimed, "Don't worry about it, Go downtown FDNY!"

They answered, "No we really should exchange information."

Meanwhile, 15 George with Yamel Marino was heading downtown with lights and siren blaring enroute to the World Trade Center to help rescue people and save lives.

In New Rochelle, New York

Deputy Chief James "J. P." Martin from the FDNY EMS, Bronx Division was home doing some chores around his house and preparing for his evening shift when the phone rang.

"Hi Chief, are we going?" Chief Martin recognized the voice as his aide, Ron.

"Going to what?" The Chief asked.

Ron replied, "A plane hit the World Trade Center. Are we going?"

Looking out the kitchen window at the clear blue sky Chief Martin thought, "How could a plane hit the World Trade Center? The building is so large how could a pilot not see the Twin Towers with great visibility. It must be a small Cessna plane." Chief Martin replied, "I will call you back Ron."

Turning on the TV Deputy Chief Martin saw the devastation and the size of the impact zone on the South Tower of the World Trade Center. Chief Martin started thinking about the fact that 50,000 people worked in the World Trade Center on a weekday and began estimating potential patient count. Suddenly the TV news showed the impact of a plane into the World Trade Center. Chief Martin wondered, "Is that an instant replay of the crash? Is that another view of the crash?"

When the TV reporter announced a plane had struck the South Tower Chief Martin realized that this was no accident and today was going to be a busy day.

Knowing terrorists often attack twice Chief Martin realized this was a terrorist attack. Chief remembered that Al Qaeda had promised they would be back to finish the devastation of the World Trade Center after the 1993 bombing and realized they meant what they said. He started running his mental checklist as he had done so many times before when considering the possibilities of a MCI. What is the potential for patients? What are the hazards? What do I know about the buildings? What is the best access? Chief Martin called his aid Ron back and said, "Ron, meet me at the Academy. I will pick you up there."

Chief Martin thought of the World Trade Center and recalled the access points, pre-designated staging locations and the control center located in the basement. Chief Martin had watched the Trade Center being built. As his family would drive from the Bronx to his father's business located in Staten Island, they would pass by the World Trade Center construction site on the way. Week by week he had watched the iconic figure of the World Trade Center rise from the ground, reaching skyward pronouncing New York's superiority and pursuit of excellence.

Earlier in his career Chief Martin had been a Lieutenant with the NYC EMS Special Operations Division (SOD). The responsibilities of the SOD supervisor were to respond to Mass Casualty Incidents and aid the local EMS supervisor in MCI management. Chief Martin became expert in unraveling tangled confusion at the scene of MCIs in the early days of EMS. MCI management was not considered a strength of EMS Lieutenants and EMS supplemented their response with a citywide SOD car to run MCIs. Chief Martin had learned how to communicate with other agencies, and learned the art of getting MCIs back on track during his time in SOD. He was well versed in establishing the priorities of MCI management. Chief Martin looked at MCIs as a big tangled ball of string. His job was to create order so patient care and transportation could be handled efficiently while keeping EMS providers safe.

Chief Martin had also been to the World Trade Center for disaster planning tours when he was a SOD supervisor and knew the layout of the buildings. He had been to the top of the Twin Towers in Windows on the World Restaurant and had flown around the Towers in an NYPD Aviation helicopter.

"New York's Best"
Lieutenant Rich Cestaro and EMT Bobby Brown, NYC EMS Special
Operations Division, with the Twin Towers in the skyline before 9/11
(Photo Courtesy of Division Chief J.P. Martin, Retired)

Chief Martin called his brother and asked, "Can you come watch the dog. I am going to work early. My wife is working a 12 hour shift." Next chief Martin called his wife and said, "I will be going downtown."

"Ok Jim, pack a bag, you remember what happened last time, you were there for 18 hours" his wife advised, referring to the 1993 bombing of the World Trade Center. She added, "Remember to bring clothes and some food, last time you were there you were there a long time."

Chief Martin Going Downtown

Chief Martin walked out to his department chief's car, a 1996 Chevrolet Caprice with the FDNY red, yellow and white color combination and the FDNY Logo on the door. Chiefs in the FDNY

EMS were allowed to take home their cars so they would be able to respond in case of just such an emergency like today.

Chief Martin is a precise individual. He is a designer by avocation and grew up working in his father's showcase design company. Chief Martin took excellent care of his car and was especially proud of the NYPD highway patrol light bar on the roof, which sported a McDermott High Rise light bar used by NYPD highway patrol cars. Chief Martin's car was the only one sporting such a light bar in the FDNY. The fact that he had a NYPD Light bar on his car within the FDNY was testament to what a detail oriented and persistent person he was. The fact that the light bar was officially installed and approved by the Chief in charge of EMS was also evidence of his widespread respect in the department. Chief Martin was a distinctive man and a distinctive leader with an eye for detail and a knack of making order out of chaos.

Chief Martin packed some batteries, a battery charger, some food and spare clothes, realizing that this could be a long day. Chief Martin drove to the Academy and picked up his aid, Ron. He turned on his light bar and motored onto the highway, turning onto the Cross Island Parkway and started towards Manhattan. He started thinking about the best way into Manhattan as they saw the smoke from the Twin Towers in the distance. On the EMS, Fire, and NYPD radios traffic was constant with information and requests for help.

A warning was issued regarding a third possible inbound plane. The FAA had information a third plane had been hijacked and turned off their transponder. Everyone was wondering where the plane was heading and if the plane was coming downtown. With the amount of rescuers on the scene a third plane crash would be horrific. Terrorist organizations were known for causing secondary attacks to attack rescuers and provide visual imagery to cause public panic and show devastation over television. The end result of terrorism is to cause fear and promote their agenda. Chief Martin thought of how he would help manage this MCI and try to keep EMS providers safe.

As Chief Martin peaked the Kosciusko Bridge on the Brooklyn Queens Expressway the electronic sign ahead read, "NEW YORK CITY CLOSED." Looking to his right Chief Martin could see the World Trade Center in the distance. He drove toward Manhattan thinking, "What are we doing. We are heading into trouble like firemen going into the burning building." He started wondering if these were military or civilian planes that hit the buildings and if they were laden with chemicals. He decided he wanted to limit exposure to EMS responders as much as possible.

Chief Martin thought the East River bridges would be jammed with people leaving Manhattan so he opted to swing downtown via Brooklyn and the Brooklyn Bridge. When he reached the Brooklyn Bridge thousands of people were fleeing Manhattan covered with ash and soot. He decided to establish a secondary staging and casualty collection point expecting hospitals in Manhattan to be overwhelmed and units would be leaving Manhattan. Chief Martin planned to triage patients and transport them to Queens, Long Island and the Bronx. He knew in a disaster of this size the local hospitals would be overwhelmed with walk-in patients.

"We can stage hundreds of resources here," he told his aid.

Chief Martin was estimating 50,000 patients, 10% may be critical and the rest may have smoke inhalation. He ordered the recall of all Haz Tac personnel to help with the large-scale exposure to dust and debris.

Haz Tac Personnel Recalled

The phone at the Battalion rang. I answered, "Hello Lt. Kanarian, Battalion 5–5."

"This is the Citywide dispatcher, we are recalling all Haz Tac personnel. Let us know when you get Haz Tac capable units to send downtown."

I responded, "10–4 got it."

Haz Tac units are EMS ambulances that do 911 calls but are equipped and trained to perform decontamination in cooperation with FDNY Haz Mat units. I knew I had Alexis at the station riding with a non-Haz Tac person. I thought, "If I could get one more Haz Tac EMT they could be sent downtown."

I called several people and got no answer. I realized Booch had to be home but ducking our call. I called him again and got his answering machine. I next decided to try his pager, I dialed his pager and at the tone left the station phone number followed by 911, 911 , 911, to stress this was an emergency not the usual call to fill an overtime vacancy.

In a few minutes the phone rang and I answered, "Battalion 5–5, Lt. Kanarian."

Booch spoke up, "Ok, I'll bite, what's the joke."

"No joke Booch, a plane has hit the World Trade Center and the Tower is on fire."

Booch replied, "No way."

"Actually Booch, there is a plane into each tower and they are both on fire."

"Bullshit." Booch quipped.

"Really, turn on the TV, you will see." I replied.

"What channel?" Booch asked.

"Any one you want, Booch." I replied. There was a pause for a few minutes.

"Ohhh, shi-it. I am on my way in. I have to take a shower, but I will be in." Booch said.

I exclaimed, "A shower are you kidding? Get in here!"

He said, "No, I have to take a shower and then I will be in. You don't understand."

I told Booch, "You and Alexis will go downtown as 17H2. Hurry up." I put down the phone and began to think about what I should be doing — what are our immediate concerns and what are some longer-term needs

10:00 A.M. Collapse of the South Tower

On the Manhattan Fire Frequency a Marine fireboat from the fire department calls fire alarm, "Marine 1 to Manhattan."....

"Marine 1 proceed"...

"Manhattan we have had a complete collapse of the South Tower. I cannot see anything except dust. The South Tower is gone."

The Manhattan Dispatcher calls out for the Field Com unit. No answer.

Chief Martin thought, "They are all dead. The hierarchy of FDNY is gone, EMS leadership is gone. I am still alive."

Realizing Chiefs he had worked with for decades were gone he put his emotions aside and realized he was still alive and had to assume command. Chief Martin thought of what Chief Zacchary Goldfarb would do. He heard Zac's voice in his mind, "Ask for a roll call of Chief Officers."

He then called the EMS Citywide Dispatcher and advised him to do a roll call of Chief Officers who were operating at the World Trade Center site. Thinking of the Chiefs he had worked with for decades, Chief Martin realized at this moment the job must go on, patients had to be treated and command had to be established. Chief Martin realized he had to return a sense of order in this catastrophe. In the background he listened for confirmation from any of the Chief Officers on the scene of the collapse of the World Trade Center, there were none.

Chief Martin realized his first job was to provide a sense of command. Through his calm and collected demeanor, Chief Martin gave direction and helped to re-establish the flow of command and sense of control as he had done countless times before when untangling MCI's. He thought, "This is just a much bigger ball of string."

For hours Chief Martin maintained a radio presence that helped to restore order to the EMS operation. In the worst times people look for leadership. Chief Martin was maintaining a radio command for people on the ground to hear and follow. His voice over the radio was a beacon of order in a sea of confusion and chaos.

At Battalion 55

About eight of us were in the office with our eyes glued to the television. McGregor came into the office and asked, "Does anyone know what's going on?"

I replied, "Yeah, I know what's going on? A plane hit the freaking World Trade Center, that's what's going on. Get your shit together, come on."

The phone was constantly ringing off the hook. "Rodriguez, take the phone," I called out.

Keith McGregor arrived and asked, "What's up Boss?"

I exclaimed, "What's up is there is a plane into each of the World Trade Towers. That is what's up."

Suddenly, we saw the antenna tower on the South Tower quiver, then lean to the side and disappear into a bank of smoke. The World Trade Center, the icon of New York City, had vanished in front of our eyes. As the South Tower sank, so did our hearts. I still remember watching the South Tower collapse on TV.

Alexis yelled out, "Oh man! This is ridiculous!"

The telephones completely stopped ringing; there was absolute silence. Then, the phones started ringing again and people were shouting with emotion in the office.

I thought, "I can't work like this."

"Everybody out!" I ordered. I turned off the TV in my office and looked at the computer dispatch screen. I saw about 40 units on the scene of the Trade Center.

I shouted, "Please, go use the TV in the kitchen. McGregor, you watch the front door. Marcus, I need you to get a handle on the extra supplies we have. Alexis, check what extra Haz Mat stuff we have in the locker. Everyone else get out!"

I thought at that moment that we probably just lost twenty to thirty EMTs and now we will be on even ground with the FD and PD. I never imagined that the fire department would have lost 340 firemen and even the department chaplain. *Never!*

I locked the door and turned the TV back on. The smoke eventually cleared enough to see Number One World Trade Center standing alone. "What the world will be like with only one World Trade Tower?" While shaking my head I thought, "How weird that will be!"

When the South Tower collapsed I looked over to the computer dispatch screen and noticed we had about forty units on the scene.

My attention turned to the Citywide radio, "Central I need help, I can, can not breath, I cannot, se–e, I need help."

I quickly thought, "Are they using weapons of mass destruction?"

The citywide dispatcher tried to give the medic direction to the nearest triage area, but it is impossible to find your way when you are in a dust cloud of darkness.

10:29 A.M. Collapse of the North Tower

We watched the television as the North Tower collapsed. "I can't believe this shit!" Alexis screamed, "This is *unre-al*!"

I directed the EMT answering the phone to tell everybody who calls to come in early.

Several EMTs were calling and checking in, saying things such as "This is EMT Pabon. I cannot come in I have child care, as soon as I can get a sitter I will be in."

When the North Tower collapsed there were no more radio transmissions because NYPD and FDNY had their radio towers on a 360 foot antenna mast on the roof of the North Tower of the World Trade Center along with ten other TV channels. Communications from Ground Zero stopped and the worst seemed to be a reality. The radio was completely silent. Dispatch was not able to reach anybody at the World Trade Center.

I called the Borough office for direction. There was no answer. I called the RCC office at 9 Metro Tech. The phone was simply dead, no busy tone, no ringing, just dead. I called Jacobi EMS Station and the Lieutenant told me, they all went downtown.

"Any direction before they left?" I asked.

The Lieutenant replied, "What can we do Steve?"

I saw one of the supervising fire marshals in the garage. I inquired about security for the station. I thought with the events of the day there might be more attacks and chaos in the streets. The supervising marshal exclaimed, "Are you kidding, we are all going downtown!"

Lt. J.J. Scotch rushed into the Battalion office, in high speed and said, "If we switch 17 Henry into vehicle 210 we can send 17 Henry with the Haz Mat crew downtown and run 66J in lieu of 17 Henry."

"J.J.," I said repeatedly motioning with my steadying hand to the door, "on days like this, chiefs want the patrol bosses on the road. I can handle this! Please go on the road."

I thought, "I can handle anything but I need calm and order." I reached down and sipped my tea. Even though it was cold I was reassured of a sense of normalcy. J.J. left to go on patrol. I knew from my experience that chiefs want patrol bosses on the road, expediting units out of the hospital and keeping our guys safe.

USAR Team Recalled

The phone rang, and I calmly answered "Lt. Kanarian, Battalion 5–5.

"Hi Lieutenant this is Jeanette from the Academy, the USAR team has been recalled by order of Operations, we need you to come to the Academy immediately."

I replied, "I am running the station, I can't just leave."

Jeanette answered, "Well, the USAR team has been recalled. You are being ordered to report to the Academy."

I said, "I am sorry, I can't leave right now. When I get relief I will come to the Academy."

She responded, "Very well, we shall see you when you get here."

"Wow!" I was floored and thought, "I am being directed to respond to the Academy but yet I am responsible for a station. If I leave who will assume responsibility for the station. Who will give the units their guidance. Who will be responsible for the equipment?"

In the background I heard the radio, "By order of the Captain all personnel are to move north of Chambers Street."

"They really need help down there." I thought, "One thing at a time. I am sure paramedics and EMTs are rushing from around the city to help. I need to get the station flowing and back on track. The station comes first."

I put an EMT on the phone. The phone kept ringing,

The EMT manning the phone advised me Lt. Periu was on the phone. I picked up the phone and said, "Hi Phil."

He asked, "What is the word, Steve?"

"Phil, the Division is empty, the line to 9 Metro Tech is dead, and we have no direction. The USAR Team has been recalled but I cannot leave."

"I am coming in. I will relieve you. Give me 50 minutes," Periu stated.

"Ok," I said as I hung up.

The phone rang again, I picked it up and heard, "This is Keith. What are we doing?"

"Come on in; bring your equipment," I told him and promptly hung up. Keith is a serious EMT. He didn't need any other instructions.

Finally EMT Booch arrived at the Battalion. By now several EMTs had reported for work. A terrible attack like this and people were coming in from home to help. We had 17 Henry return and unload their personal equipment. I paired up Booch and Alexis on the Haz Tac unit and got them in service to respond downtown.

EMTs lined up, asking to go to the disaster site to help.

EMT Roberts proclaimed "Lt. Kanarian, I want to go with them"

I said, "Ok, get in."

Another EMT asked "Can I go also?"

I replied, "No, stay here you're an asthmatic."

Margaret said, "I want to go."

I told her, "No you're a single mother."

Jason asked to go. I said, "Yes you can go EMT Hagar."

We loaded the extra weapons of mass destruction antidote kits and Scott Air Pak bottles in the vehicle. I closed the door and knocked on the side; I looked forward to the cab and gave the thumbs up to Booch.

Keith walked up to the ambulance and shook hands with Booch. No words where said. They understood each other with a quick look. They knew the gravity of the situation and were speaking as partners do, non-verbally.

As 17 Henry left the sunlight filled the garage bay and a feeling of emptiness came over me. I thought, "What did I just do? I just sent five single guys downtown to the World Trade Center where terrorists are possibly using weapons of mass destruction. This is a war zone. What did I do?" I honestly did not know if I would ever see them alive again. I thought "This must be what it was like in Vietnam when a fighter plane left the carrier for a mission. They might come back, or they might not. That was war." I really did not know if I would see those guys again.

In all the training we have had I never had considered making those decisions I just made in a minutes time. How did I make those decisions? Looking back I realize that my ability to make those decision in the moment was the culmination of all my training and experience as a medic, supervisor and USAR Medical Specialist.

I returned to the office and sat in the chair. Then, I heard someone say, "Berrios is on the phone for you, Sir."

I answered saying, "Berrios, what's up brother?"

He replied, "Lieutenant, I am in the World Financial Center. I am treating seven critical patients and five minor patients. I need help Lt. Kanarian."

"Josh, I don't know if I can get you help."

"Lieutenant, I am alone and without equipment, I was down here for family court. I need somebody to help me. I don't even have a radio!"

"Ok, ok, Josh. Tell me the building you're in, tell me the floor, the cubicle and the phone nearest to you. I will try to get you help."

Knowing the problems we have on normal days finding patients in large office buildings I figured with the right information I could possibly get help to him.

Josh gave his location "I am in room…"

As Josh gives me the floor and room number, I think "What the hell is communications going to say when I call? Can I possibly help this EMT in a dire situation down there. It must be total chaos downtown. I don't know. This day is out of control.

"O.K. Josh, I will try to get you help. Hang on, Brother," I advised him, "Do not move from that location."

The phone rang and I heard, "Hi this is Sylvia. I can't reach my daughter. She...she is downtown. She works near the Trade Center."

I could hear the tremble in her voice as Sylvia thought the worst. She was probably thinking, My God is my daughter alive? She asked, "Has she called the station?"

I replied, "No Sylvia, I haven't heard from her." I thought, "This is not EMS business, and then I thought this is a fellow Lieutenant trying to find her daughter, trying to communicate."

"My daughter works downtown. I am trying to find her. If she calls let her know I am ok. Find out where she is."

I said, "Will do Sylvia."

I began to write the recent events in the logbook. I thought back to the events of the past hour and wondered what really had to go in the book. I began to realize that communication was important, continuous communication was important. Looking through the logbook would not do when I left to go downtown.

I posted a summary of people and equipment both on and off duty and who were downtown for accountability. I thought a newsgroup kind of message would be better for each person. I took a pad and placed a name on the top. As phone calls came in I added the next message under the first. This way a lieutenant or captain could quickly follow each group of messages.

The phone yelped interrupting my thoughts. "Hi, H-i-iii my mom is a lieutenant at this station. A shaky voice asked, "Is Sylvia working today? I am her," cough, cough "her daughter."

I told her, "Thank goodness you are Ok. Your mom is downtown looking for you. She is ok. How are you?"

She responded, "I am ok, too. I am going home, walking south to Brooklyn. I will keep trying her cell, nothing is working."

I said "Good, stay clear and watch yourself, get home. I will tell your mother you're ok." I immediately called Sylvia, reassured her that her daughter was alive and what I had told her daughter.

I called Citywide dispatch. "I have an EMT in the World Financial Center with seven critical patients."

"I can't make any promises. Where is he?" I gave the location, his shield number #4109 and the name EMT Josh Berryman. I added, "I went to the Academy with Josh Berryman."

"I will try, Lieutenant." I make a log entry and note the time and the dispatcher I spoke to.

"Boss, Matonis is on the phone," EMT Smith shouted out to me. "Lieutenant, what should I do."

I answered, "Mike, we have enough help. Stay home."

He replied, "I have to help. I was a US Army Ranger. We lead the way. I am not saying home."

"Mike all the bridges are closed. Go to the closest station, Battalion 49. Report to the Lieutenant there and tell them you spoke to me." I recorded Mike Matonis on the board and in the log, another one of our guys going downtown. At least after I leave people will know he is working in Queens and not missing for work.

Ralph Winburn called on the phone and said, "L-T, I want to help."

I answered, "Stay home Ralph. They have enough help and Hell is breaking loose downtown. And the bridges are all closed."

He exclaimed, "L-T, I have to help!"

I replied, "OK Ralph. Go to Battalion 49 and I will let them know you are coming. Matonis is also going there."

I realized I should call home and speak with my wife, Moira, a reired NY police officer.

"I am going downtown, unless you don't want me to." I said.

"I may not be on the job anymore but I am trained for this. I will watch the kids; go downtown and help."

I had called home, half hoping she would say, do not go. It was a shaky feeling thinking about going downtown. Then I remembered the others and they needed help. I heard the voices on the radio.

Moira said, "Go downtown, it is ok, I will take care of everything at home."

I stopped and thought, "Maybe I should not go down there, to that war zone."

I again heard the voices on the radio calling for help and in obvious distress. I thought, "I have to go help our own."

IV

Express Bus to Ground Zero.
Tuesday September 11, 2001

I felt relieved to turn over station operations to another Lieutenant; the pace of the station was like a locomotive traveling full steam ahead. My mind was on getting downtown and making a difference. I was thinking, "I can now focus on helping at Ground Zero where help was desperately needed. Surely hundreds of people are injured and trapped who need emergency care. News reports said all bridges and tunnels in and out of Manhattan were closed."

The EMS system was stretched to the limits dealing with the collapse of the Twin Towers and the 911 call volume. Spare ambulances were being pressed into service with EMTs and paramedics who were coming into work after the recall of all off-duty FDNY personnel. The City was in shock; the City was like a prize boxer who got the wind knocked out of him, down on one knee. The usual support and chain of command operations were focusing on downtown. Phone lines to headquarters were not working. The division office was empty because everyone went downtown.

I called Station 20 and spoke to the desk Lieutenant. I asked him if they had any transportation to the Academy.

"Come on up here Steve we will get you to the Academy," replied the Lieutenant. I said "Thanks. See you in a while."

11:30 A.M. Heading to the Academy

I got a ride to Jacobi Hospital and met Lieutenant Polk from Division 20 who offered to give me a quick ride over the bridge to the Academy. The uncertainty was palpable while driving toward the Whitestone Bridge on the expressway. I made some small talk to work out the anxiety I was now feeling about going downtown. I did a mental checklist of my equipment, "helmet, safety coat, gloves and goggles." I usually kept a few bottles of water and granola bars in my bag in case I was on an MCI for a long time. I would probably need that water tonight. We approached the Whitestone Bridge toll plaza and the traffic was completely stopped. A police officer stepped forward and motioned for us to stop. EMS relations with the NYPD are usually good, but you never know when a problem will arise.

"Going downtown Lieutenant?" the police officer inquired.

Steve Polk replied, "Yes we are."

I thought briefly, "I hope he isn't going to try to stop us from crossing the bridge."

The officer said, "Have a safe trip. I understand they need medics down there." He turned to the toll booth attendant and motioned to raise the gate.

"Godspeed gentlemen" the Triboro Bridge and Tunnel Officer said.

I looked to my right as we crossed the Whitestone Bridge. I saw LaGuardia Airport in the foreground and the skyline of Manhattan in the background. The skyline of Manhattan was filled with whitish-grey smoke billowing towards Brooklyn. The smoke looked like some wild beast that had claimed its victim and was now reeling to protect its prey.

"Shit!" I thought, "This is for real. This is not some bad dream."

We drove around the exit ramp and approached Fort Totten. Two Military Police with M-16's were guarding the gate. They looked at our marked fire department vehicle and directed us to stop.

"Sir we need to see ID. Please open the trunk." They peered in the trunk and back seat, and then came back up to the driver's door.

"Wow!" I thought, "This was different from the usual private security guard waving us through from the sitting position in the guard house."

The MP raised his hand to his head in a formal military salute form and motioned for us to pass entering Fort Totten.

In front of the EMS Academy the refresher students and new employee class were being lined up in front to ride downtown to help with patient care. Mobilization of EMS Academy personnel and students was a part of the doomsday MCI plan. Staff and supervisors were so busy and intent on what they were doing that we moved by and into the Academy without being noticed. I went into the lobby.

"Kanarian. How are you? What brings you here?" asked Joey

I replied, "I am heading downtown."

Joey said, "The USAR team left about ninety minutes ago. Where were you?"

I answered, "I had to get relief at the station."

He said, "Check with the Chief's secretary. She is in touch with Operations."

I walked down the hall to the secretary's office. As I approached her desk I greeted her, "Hi. How are you?"

The Chiefs secretary looked at me blankly, "They're all gone."

"What do you mean?" I asked.

"They are all gone," she continued, "there is a list of two hundred missing employees."

"You mean fire and EMS?" I asked. "No." She said, "Just EMS. They don't even have a number of how many firefighters are missing. They are all gone."

"Can I see the list?" I asked.

"No." She blurted shaking her hand back and forth reaffirming her no answer. I saw the sorrow in her eyes and could not imagine who was on the list. Quietly she told me a few names, "Chief McCracken, the Chief of Department Ganci and SOC Chief Downey — they are all gone."

Goose bumps formed on the back of my neck and arms. My chest was moist with sweat. I felt nauseous. The magnitude of the loss was difficult to comprehend. I thought, "I have to get down there and help. We are trained for this; we know how to help entrapped patients. I have to get downtown."

I looked down at her computer and saw a picture of the Brooklyn Bridge on her desktop screen. In the background was the World Trade Center and in the foreground was a picture of an EMS ambulance.

"Wow! What a stark contrast now," I thought. A common photo now had uncommon significance and would never be seen again like that.

Riverview of New York Skyline with Twin Towers in 1989

The World Trade Center was a pillar of this city and a part of the fabric of New York. It was hard to believe a landmark as important to us as the World Trade Center is gone. It was like a 200-year old oak, the pillar of your neighborhood and a cornerstone of your life, had been uprooted by a storm. Actually it was like the bully around the bend that resented you and everything you stood for had come and ripped the tree up and tore up your roots and sense of being. A shot out of the dark, the Twin Towers are gone, so are all our big Chiefs.

"Let's get you downtown," the secretary said. "I will have the van drop you off at Metropolitan where you can pick up a USAR medic. From there they will give you a bus to go downtown."

Bus is a colloquial New York term for ambulance. "Rush the bus" is a common expression among police officers.

World Trade Center Front Doors before 9/11

"Thank you." I said. I reached out for her hand; I held her hand and squeezed. She appeared as though her mind was in a faraway place. Her hands were cold and she looked off to the side.

As I loaded my equipment on to the van I thought about how close the senior administration were. Together they had worked on ambulances and worked their way up the ladder to the top. I am sure they had differences day-to-day but in a time like this differences erode and we realized how much we truly cared for one another. Bad times always bring out the best in people.

I picked up the USAR Medic at Metropolitan Hospital. We headed out of the gate and saw a barrage of construction equipment on the FDR. A column of pay loaders and backhoes were driving in a procession downtown filled the FDR. Occasionally the line was broken by several ten-wheel construction dump trucks. We turned onto Second Avenue and met with heavy traffic.

At the next intersection a NYPD cadet dressed in grey came forward and saluted. "Lieutenant, I suggest you turn right at 90th street and get on Broadway. Broadway is reserved for emergency vehicles."

I thanked the cadet and began to maneuver the bus as he said, "stay safe." He tapped the hood of the ambulance twice.

We maneuvered down Second Avenue then over to 90th Street, which was a one-way street. We scooted down the block; "Whooop, whoop, whoop," chirped the siren. People were actually yielding right of way to the ambulance; cars were pushing up onto the curb.

Today was different! Everybody understood this was an emergency that affected everyone; it was not the usual medical emergency that affected one person in private. Today the attack on the Twin Towers made everybody realize we were all facing a common enemy together.

Upon reaching Broadway an officer waived us on and pointed south and said, "Stay safe EMS, God bless."

I looked at the officer and thought, "Shit, I have never heard an officer tell me God bless." I realized we are really heading down into harm's way. I wondered what we would find there.

We traveled down Broadway with our lights and siren on. Police officers and Academy cadets had closed every block. We drove non-stop downtown. Occasionally I would see a freeze frame of a person on a corner. A person dumbstruck and fearful, a police officer saluting us, then a woman making the sign of the cross as we drove by in the bus. I saw an EMT from New York Presbyterian riding his bike downtown. We were all getting downtown to help whoever we could.

I thought, "This is the big job!"

As we approached Canal Street I stopped and saw traffic everywhere. I was not sure which way to turn. I looked up through the top of the windshield, first left, then right. I peered trying to look further downtown.

Vinnie asked, "What are you looking for?"

I turned to him and said "the Trade Center."

He said, "They are gone Steve, try a left and a quick right. That block looks clear."

Looking for the Twin Towers was a natural way of getting oriented in lower Manhattan. Looking for the Twin Towers today reminded me of being a kid and turning on the light switch when there was no power. It was a reflex; the Towers were part of the City and our lives, now they were gone. Instinctively I was looking for the Twin Towers for a sense of direction and to get a feel of how close we were. The Twin Towers were not only an icon that was the soul of New York City's greatness but they provided a beacon we used to find our direction.

I turned left, then over the curb. A loud "Bang!" filled the air and a vibration shuddered through the frame of the bus. Our ambulance bottomed out on a concrete median but we kept going. I hit the gas and we shot through the intersection down a block. Next thing I knew we were in a dustbowl near Chambers Street; it was deadly quiet and everything was covered with dust.

1:30 P.M. Arriving at Ground Zero

All of a sudden we were at Ground Zero. We could see the cinder grey smoke curdling above the site. People covered in dust were walking around, going nowhere, some peered into the sky. A man sat on the corner with his arms around his knees looking at the ground. Motionless, he stared straight ahead. A police officer was restraining a man who wanted to go past the barricade screaming, "My mother is in there. I have gotta go help!"

I saw a Chief's car coming by. I motioned for them it to stop, and I asked the Chief, "Where is staging?"

The Chief, who was covered in ash and dust, looked through me into the distance. "I repeated, "Chief where is the USAR Team staging?" I got no reply or acknowledgment.

The Captain in the passenger seat leaned across and said, "Steve, Chambers and West Street is the EMS Command Post. They will know where USAR is staging."

"Thanks Sir." I replied. Looking at the expression in the Chief's eyes I wondered, "What have they seen?"

The Chief looked ahead and the Crown Victoria car sped away.

We drove to West Street and turned left; long down the horizon was Ground Zero. There was grayish white smoke rolling over itself and moving toward the Hudson River. Along with that there was tangy taste of dust in the air, a taste of drywall or lime.

**Ground Zero After the Collapse of the Twin Towers
(Photo Courtesy of Luis Matallana)**

I looked to my left and saw ambulance 485 parked on the north side of West Street with the emergency lights and the engine off, just like we are supposed to do. Good Medics always point their vehicle away from the scene toward the closest trauma center. Saint Vincent's would be the closest. The goal is to get your patient to transport and get them to the trauma center without getting blocked in traffic.

I recognized vehicle 485; it is Four-Nine Victor's Ambulance from my old station in Queens, Battalion 49. Carlos Lillo worked that Unit Tour 2. I wondered, "Is he here?"

As I approached the command post I saw Chief McCracken. I was very glad to see that he had survived.

I walked up to him and said, "Hi Chief. How are you?"

"I have had better days," he replied.

I asked the Chief "Where is USAR staging?"

"Chambers and West," he replied.

Chief McCracken was a natural leader. I noticed as the Chief walked away he was covered in soot and seemed to wince in pain with each step.

"Chief, are you ok?" I inquired.

He answered, "Yes. I have some more things to do before I get checked out."

When he was the Chief of the Bronx, there was a palpable command presence when he was in the borough of the Bronx.

I thought, "I am glad he is alive. He is still a leader to look up to on the worst day in our city's history."

I walked down Chambers Street and saw the tractor-trailer with USAR equipment in Anvil boxes. On my right I saw a fire engine that was idling on the corner. The truck was covered in dust on the outside and the inside. The inside of the truck was covered with dust in an unnatural way; the inside of the windshield was dusty, the computer was dusty, and the seats and the dashboard were covered in dust as was *The New York Post* on the dashboard.

I kept walking down Chambers Street and saw some familiar faces. I entered the corner lot and joined the group.

I saw Doctor Gonzalez and asked him, "What is the plan, Doc?"

He replied, "Nobody knows yet. We are waiting for word."

As I looked around I noticed an absence of forward direction, no plan of action. I had never been to a job in New York City and felt this kind of vacuum. Hundreds of survivors were working on their knees using only their hands to find their co-workers and people who worked in the building. The collapse of the Twin Towers had left a huge void in the command structure. Especially hard hit was the SOC and USAR team. Members of the USAR team were standing waiting for direction.

In the background was silence. I looked around the block and saw there was no electricity, no traffic, only dust swirling through the air. I thought, "Wow! This is not the Manhattan I know, the one that is usually congested with traffic, bubbling with everyday excitement of being in the greatest city in the world."

In the backdrop I heard a fire department officer saying, "As it stands now we have lost all of the SOC units, Chief of Department Ganci and Chief Downey."

**FDNY members of USAR Team at the Staging Area on 9/11
(Photo Courtesy of Luis Matallana)**

A lot of these guys were the infrastructure and lead roles of the USAR team. Chief Downey was a widely respected rescue operations chief who spoke around the country and published articles and books. He was the kind of chief everyone looked up to on a job like this. But now Chief Downy and the Twin Towers were both gone.

I could not help thinking, "New York is like a boxer down on the mat, resting on one knee, the wind knocked out of him, the referee counting: one, two, three… Our city was like a prizefighter that was stunned. Down and out."

I had never been to a response in New York City were there was not a sense of forward motion and knowledge of the next thing to do. The group stood around chatting and guessing how many rescue personnel were lost and wondering if anyone was still alive.

A fireman addressed us saying, "By now the surface rescues are done. We have to find the voids and look for survivors. The weather is favorable for survivors. If they have water and it does not get too cold they can last a day or two. Let's get down there and get digging!"

The fireman called out, "We need to start thinking about the long term operation, preparing for the next couple of weeks. The guys on the pile will be getting tired late tonight. We have to set up and prepare for a prolonged operation. We are here until the end until we pull everyone out, one way or another."

5:25 P.M. Collapse of Number 7 World Trade Center

In the distance a loud rumbling was heard like a roller coaster. "Number Seven is going. Run!" someone yelled.

Everybody looked up and froze for a millisecond.

A salient voice spoke, "Do not run. We are far enough away. We're ok. We do not run brothers. We are the FDNY. Look down and close your eyes."

As the rumbling ceased a tinkling sound passed over us as dust settled to the ground, the sky darkened, small pieces of soot and debris deposits fluttered over us. I wiped the back of my neck and slowly looked up. A ray of sunshine was piercing the dust cloud.

I thought, "That building was about 10 stories high." Later I was to learn that Seven World Trade Center was a 47-story building. The collapse of Number 7 World Trade Center happened in about 3 seconds.

The collapse of this building served as an exclamation point on an already unbelievable day. The collapse of Number 7 World Trade Center happened at 5:25 p.m.

Number 7 World Trade Center Collapsing
(Photo Courtesy of Luis Matallana)

**Pandemonium after the Collapse of the Twin Towers
(Photo Courtesy of Luis Matallana)**

The air cleared and there was a gap in the skyline where Number 7 World Trade Center had been. As if the days events where not already enough, we had to experience the loss of another building. I guess it was fate's way of telling us to get moving, there is a lot of work to be done.

Number 7 World Trade Center on the Ground
(Photo Courtesy of Bobby Wong)

Setting up USAR Medical Base Camp

Within the group leaders emerged. One of the USAR team members directed, "Guys lets unload the cache and set up the tents. Gloves are a must when handling the Anvil boxes. We are here to the end; we don't need any more injuries. Let's get this done."

We unpacked the tents and USAR equipment box by box. We now had a sense of forward direction. Right then I realized, "We are going to get this job done."

As our group began setting up USAR operations in our shocked condition, I wondered "What drives people in these situations?" I mentally compared our actions to the human heart, which is blessed with the property of automaticity. The heart has an inherent ability to stimulate contractions on its own. When the sinoatrial node fails to discharge electricity and cause a synchronized contraction the next pacemaker, the Atrioventricular node (AV), will fire. In the event the AV node does not fire, the ventricles will fire and begin contraction to continue blood flow and the action of pumping blood.

The moment of Number 7 World Trade Center collapsed was like a sole pacemaker impulse stimulating the heart to begin beating again. The left ventricle was the strong part of the heart and capable of pumping blood to the body. As one cell beats the action potential spreads to the rest of the myocardium and a synchronized effort begins, much like what was happening with the rescuers coming to help the survivors look for their partners, friends and family members. I had the feeling we were starting the long-term operation and priming the heart of New York City, and maybe the country.

One by one we unloaded the boxes and identified which sector the boxes went in: logistics, medical tent, supplies, medical backpacks and so on. One by one, man to man the boxes where unloaded and passed to the next guy. We gathered around the basketball court of the schoolyard we were in and assembled the tents.

A pole here, a fastener, the canvas slipped off. Slowly the process emerged. OK, assemble the top, thread the tent lift and then add the sides. One pole after the next went up and the tent rose from the ground. The smell of the new canvas tent was a refreshing change from the dust and odor in the air. Several tents went up and the medical specialists assembled in the medical tent. Usually two doctors and four medics went on a USAR deployment. Today the whole team was ready to help. We would all function as one team.

Captain Booth began assigning shifts. Pointing to each group he said, "You guys help set up camp, you four set up your equipment, and you will be ready in case we have to scramble a team for a rescue."

I thought, "Just as a heart that had stopped beating slowly finds an escape beat or two then a junctional rhythm, new pacemakers were emerging and we were getting into a mode of operation." The usual barrage of plans and printed orders were missing; we have to do the whole thing on our own. One by one we started establishing a routine and working toward preparing for the downwind walk.

I looked over and saw my good friend Jay Swithers sitting on some boxes looking defeated and distant. I asked, "What's wrong Jay?"

"I am not having a good month Steve. I mean it is ok in the sense that I was promoted to Captain but I can't believe the Towers are gone. I don't even know what happened and I was standing right here. I saw the Tower collapsing and I felt the urge to run. I told myself that I had to be brave and set a good example; I am after all, a new Captain. Then I saw a Chief run by, he yelled, 'Rrrrun Jay, run.' Then I figured my reaction was the right one. I could not see anything and there was complete silence. I was not sure if I was blind or dead. I did not know which way to go. I was thinking about my kids...what life would be like without their dad. I could not breathe the air was so thick with dust. Someone grabbed my helmet, then shouted, 'A fireman, he will know what to do!' I didn't know what to do. I was as confused as they were. I told him to hold on and follow me."

I did not know what to say. I reached out and put my hand on Jay's shoulder.

"Are you injured Jay?" I inquired.

"No. I'm just having a bad month. Earlier this month I had a call for a van with a family of five that died when hit by a drunk driver."

I responded, "Jay, you need a vacation brother."

Jay just looked off at the ground and returned to his thoughts of the events of the day. I could see he needed some time alone to rest. I got him a bottle of water and Jay just held the bottle.

Turning it and peeling at the label a small strip each time he turned and said, "Steve, I was taking care of a woman who was short of breath and burned from the impact of the plane into the towers. I sensed it was time to move out of the courtyard between the towers; the crowd kept getting smaller and smaller until there were only a few patients and one other EMT. I did not have a stretcher or a chair. I was debating if I should walk her or get a chair and come back. But we are trained never to walk a patient who is short of breath. Suddenly she got up, adjusted her bloomers and dress which had ridden up on her legs while sitting on the ground and she ran."

Jay shot upright and had a funny expression on his face and added, "She ran with the oxygen tank attached until the non-rebreather fell off her face. I ran after her and the Twin Towers rumbled to the ground."

"Jay, I am glad you're OK man," I replied.

I was amazed at the events Jay had experienced. I could relate to his feelings. As a paramedic we see so much tragedy sometimes it is hard to comprehend what we see and process the loss.

Captain Jimmy Booth entered the tent with a clipboard. Captain Booth looked business-like and his turnout gear was adjusted perfectly. We had all been issued a protective coat for rain and identification but guys like Captain Booth go the extra mile by having their coats tailored, installing the radio pocket on the coat and purchasing matching bunker pants.

"Damn! He always looks good," I thought.

"I need someone to pick up drugs from the command post. They have a cache of narcs (narcotics) for the team. We need a team to check the supplies for damage and begin assembling the backpacks to go down to the pile. Let's get organized, enough sitting around" the Captain said with sarcastic smirk. The slight joke made us feel a little bit more familiar and back to the normal routine, if that as ever possible again.

Then he said, "Kanarian, give me a hand."

I asked, "What's up Jimmy?"

"I am setting up a desk and a logbook. Help me move this table. I can't just sit around and wait; at least I can set up operations for us. I am opening a log book and a radio book to account for equipment and provide a log of our actions. Good deal, here let's move this over, Thanks Buddy."

"No problem Jimmy," I said, "I will go pick up the drugs at the command post."

Do you really want all that responsibility for that amount of Hooch?" he asked.

"I don't mind. I was ALS Coordinator in Queens, I am used to moving drugs around." I replied.

I walked to the command post and obtained the narcs from the citywide ALS coordinator. I remarked, "Quite a site."

"Yes it is," she said. "I got a lot to do, sign here. Now they are your responsibility."

I walked back to the tent and when I entered the activity had changed. People were checking equipment, setting up battery chargers and preparing to go down to the pile. There was a sense of business being done. Although today was different from any other day we had at work, some familiar patterns were emerging and putting us back in the groove.

While standing by the doorway I heard, "Out of the way coming through," as Captain Quigley walked up to the door with a bucket of water and a brush.

"What are you doing Jack? Are you going to clean the whole site on your own?" I smirked.

He replied, "No. I don't care what anyone says, I cannot stand a messy tent. We are going to have a boot wash station right out there by the door. Stop and put turnout gear there on the bench. Wash boots here" he said pointing to the bucket of water, "Then enter here" he said pointing to the door with the brush. "We are going to be here a long time, this tent will stay clean."

A team member squeezed by and whispered, "He is like this whenever we go camping, don't piss in his tent."

I asked Jack, "Where did you get the bucket and the brush?"

"I commandeered the bucket from a street vendor and got the brush at the Ninety-Nine Cent Store," replied Captain Quigley.

I thought, "Wow! This must really be important to Captain Jack."

We got through the unknown by the basic skills and experiences that each of us had despite having no experience similar to the World Trade Center attack. Not even the World Trade Center bombing in 1993 came close to being this bad. One by one each team members talents emerged, the whole team was coming together, and the tent and boxes now looked like a mobile medical center prepared to receive patients with injuries. We also blocked off a private area in back so medics could rest and rehydrate away from the public entrance.

The Medics continued to check equipment, set up packs, which are grey bags with zipper compartments you could adjust for each mission. Guys were filling their bags and checking drugs. I cheated. I brought six bags of fluid; IV drip sets needles syringes and just a few drugs, pre-filled syringes of epinephrine, atropine and some lido. I don't have a monitor, and chances are the lido will be used by a doc to stitch someone up. I want a light bag for the long shift ahead.

I ask the group standing around, "Anybody know how long we are going out for?"

No reply.

I figured if we had a cardiac arrest of a victim it would be pronounced anyway. If a member went down I could start the resuscitation and then call for back up with a monitor. I did not want to carry unnecessary equipment around for the hours we would be searching.

Finally, we had established our medical base camp. As much as we had to get downtown to the pile, it was necessary to realize that this was going to be a long-term rescue effort. The firefighters and police officers who had survived the collapse and who were digging in the rubble for survivors by hand would be good for another eight hours or so. We had to prepare to provide and maintain an organized medical coverage for the duration of the rescue effort. After we had assembled our equipment and established a medical base tent, we all regrouped.

As I looked around the tent I saw we had an inventory of our equipment, had set up a medical treatment area and established an area for medical specialists to sit, rehydrate and store equipment. Most of all Captain Jack was happy his tent was clean. We established a boot wash and a bench for turnout gear to be left outside.

Jack seemed happy with what we had accomplished and exclaimed, "This will work!"

**New York Task Force 1, Medical Specialists at
Medical Base Camp on 9/11
(Photo Courtesy of Luis Matallana)**

Front Row sitting, left to right: Jack Quigley, and Luis Matallana.
Middle Row, left to right: John Nevins, Dr. Aseada, Team Medical
Director Dr. Dario Gonzales, Rob Raheb, Dave Russell, Carl
Tramontana, Jay Swithers, and Steve Kanarian.
Back Row, left to right: Jeff Quigley, Gerry Santiago, Dr. Cherson,
Vinnie Johnson, and James Booth.

V

Taking the Downwind Walk.
Tuesday September 11, 2001

What enables cops, firefighters, EMTs, and paramedics to do the job we do is the knowledge that if something does go wrong, if something happens, that everyone of my brothers and sisters is going to be coming for me. And knowing that they would be coming for me, obliges me to do all that I can to come for them.

— Pat Bahnken, President of Local 2507
Uniform EMTs and Paramedics

Preparing to Go Downwind

Later on, Captain Carl Tramontana called us together and told us that they were still putting together plans of how to utilize us. He said, "For now we were going to take a downwind walk."

This was an unusual procedure for us. EMTs and paramedics are taught to go uphill from fluid spills and upwind from fumes during a Haz Mat incident. The downwind walk is the walk that Haz Mat personnel take to check out the hot zone. Haz Mat rescuers walk into harms way to assess the damage, product type or hazards and estimate the resources needed to mitigate an incident.

This time we would be walking downwind and into Ground Zero to get a first hand view of what had happened. Of course we all wanted to go rushing down there, but order and accountability of rescue personnel was essential. We had to work as a team in concert with the Command post.

As we made our final preparations, we secured our backpacks, and I clipped a flashlight to my turnout gear. I did not want to be caught in some dark corridor with no light. I fastened my respiratory filter mask to make it airtight.

**EMTs Bobby Wong and Daniel Huie
in Respiratory Filter Masks at Ground Zero
(Photo Courtesy of Bobby Wong)**

"Funny," I thought, "this seemed a lot like my first time SCUBA diving. Suiting up, making sure I had respiratory protection and wondering what kind of strange environment I was forcing myself to go into." I wondered, "What would I find? What would I see?"

9:00 P.M. Navigating Fallen I-Beams
Enroute to Ground Zero

West Street was blocked by wreckage at the North footbridge. Fire apparatus had sought refuge under the footbridge and was crushed by the collapsing Twin Towers. We walked out of the base camp and down Chambers Street; the walk to the Trade Center was about three blocks. The walk ordinarily would take about ten minutes to get down there.

Wreckage of 7 World Trade Center at the North Footbridge on 9/11

As we approached 7 World Trade Center we saw the wreckage of the Tower flat on the ground at the end of Greenwich Street. A ladder company was directing the master stream from its bucket into the fire that burned under 7 World Trade Center.

We backtracked and headed east to West Broadway to go around the wreckage. We went around the debris and were faced with pile after pile of sharp I-beams and steel that had fallen when the Twin Towers collapsed. The angular position of the steel I-beams was difficult to navigate because they were so smooth and at odd angles. It was hard to get traction to walk over the beams.

The walk over the debris was painstakingly arduous and slow. Each step was a chore, finding firm wreckage to step on, finding the right angle, and then looking for the next step. Flat portions of the ground were covered with strips of metal and other hazards.

While passing Saint Paul's Chapel we saw the graves from centuries past, which were now covered with dust from the collapse. There was a large amount of shoes in the cemetery, which seemed odd. I wondered, "Where did all these shoes come from?"

Eventually Lou and I worked our way down to Liberty and Church Street. We passed Engine 10 and Ladder 10's quarters, referred to as the Ten-Ten house. We continued to walk around the pile and found our way to the south footbridge on West Street. The scene on West Street was a dust-covered junkyard, with destroyed fire trucks and ambulances. It looked like a bone yard for emergency vehicles.

I looked towards the World Financial Center and saw a large twenty story building on fire. FDNY had some rookie firefighters called "probies" (short for probational firefighters) who are in their first year on the job working on an adjacent building pointing some hoses out the window and dousing the fire to prevent the spread to another building.

I thought, "Any other day that in itself would be a five alarm fire. Today, this fire was more of an inconvenience than an emergency unto itself. Like the kids say in the Bronx, *'This shit is off the hook!'*"

**Destroyed Ambulance in Wreckage of Twin Towers
(Photo courtesy FEMA/Andrea Booher)**

Along this field were countless fire department trucks, support vehicles, ambulances and police cars. This was very different from anything we had ever seen before. We had all seen mass casualties but in this disaster we were the victims. We were devastated! This one hit close to home, this one hit our own.

We continued walking and came upon what seemed to have been a fitness club. Captain Carl walked into the fitness club on the ground floor and looked around at the equipment. I looked around the room and saw the dust covered exercise bikes and dumbbells that were neatly placed on their shelf. There was a dust covered towel and water bottle next to the bike.

I thought, "Someone left in a hurry." It was easy to imagine the executives who were in here working out on this beautiful day when life was interrupted.

Then Captain Carl looked down and picked up a metal plaque that read "Exercise Room World Financial Center." I think he found this plaque interesting because he was an exercise buff and competitive weightlifter. After looking at the plaque Captain Carl tossed it into the rubble; we all continued walking.

Somehow the things we once thought were important and interesting had been subverted by the tragic events of the day. This workplace of the best people in finance and business had been turned into a battlefield with wreckage and bodies completely covering the area.

We found ourselves on West Street looking into the mammoth pile of debris in front of us. Pay loaders were driving over steel wires and long thin bands of aluminum that snapped and reeled like the last bite of a large serpent. Pieces of metal were sticking into their solid rubber tires as they cleared a path to begin lifting debris and looking for voids.

The night air was cool. The night was filled with sounds of excavator vehicles engines and the occasional chatter of a frustrated jackhammer unable to get purchase in the steel to begin to erode its foe.

The prospect of going in to rescue patients was overshadowed by the frank inhospitable and forbidding nature of the scene. The scene looked like a movie of the post-apocalyptic war zone. Machines with headlights were taking on the metal and steel. No place for a human on foot.

I wondered, "How could anyone survive in there if we cannot even walk into the collapse area?"

Pieces of the characteristic facade of the World Trade Center stuck upright out of West Street where they had fallen and stuck into the ground. I thought these pieces of the facade were kind of close to the road, I remembered them positioned differently. No, it had fallen into the street and stuck into the ground. Each piece had to be over one hundred feet in length.

A seven-story piece of facade fell into the street. I thought, "What a scene it must have been when this thing came down! One hundred and ten stories of steel raining down on the streets and people below." I wondered, "How could anyone survive this falling debris?"

The piles of debris were not concrete constructed walls that we usually would have found voids under during a building collapse. These piles were I-beams that left no room for any living thing; I- beams that were labeled in spray paint "4 tons" by construction workers during the assembly of the Towers.

Looking into the pit behind the façade was a dark smoky area that looked like Hell itself. The face of the Tower, what was left there, was burned and had a rusted brown color with smoke curling in the background. It looked like the pictures you would see of London after World War II in the movies.

The destruction was total and apocalyptic. I had only been to the Trade Center a couple of times, but there was nothing recognizable left of it.

I thought, "The only thing as bad as this was London in 1944, but this is Manhattan in the year 2001; we are not at world war, at least not officially."

At this point I realized that finding a live victim would be hard in this environment. The image of rescuing people and starting IVs to rehydrate patients and firemen who were trapped in the rubble was replaced by the sharp pains in my feet as we tried to maintain a level stance on this sea of metal and debris. I could feel hope dissipating in the cool fall evening with the passing breeze that chilled my exposed skin.

As the night slipped away the sound of firemen's Pass Alarms, which screeched out loud whenever a fireman stopped moving for too long, was replaced by the constant chatter or diesel engines straining, and the chatter of jackhammers not making progress, but unable to get purchase to start fix the steel below. The jackhammers were just bouncing off the steel.

We spent the rest of the night doing a recon of the area and trying to make sense of the wreckage. Captain Jack kept saying, "If we can find the gold globe we can get our bearings."

The gold globe was an icon of the Word Trade Center but it was nowhere to be found in this wreckage. It was hard to figure out where things were in comparison to where they belonged. Late at night we returned to the base camp to rest and prepare for another day of search and rescue. Surely in the daylight we will we will find voids and start rescuing people.

We worked our way back around to the base camp over our trail of metal I-beams, debris and wreckage. Step-by-step, pile by pile, we slowly made our way back to the base camp where we were greeted by some sandwiches and water bottles the Red Cross provided. It felt good to sit down and relax for a while. I suddenly realized I had not eaten since breakfast yesterday morning.

As the sun rose over Manhattan in long streaks of yellow light, the buildings around the World Trade Center looked dark and grim. One would think that the Towers would fall and not reach the other buildings. As I was looking over the site, however, I was daunted by how every building around Ground Zero had some massive scarring to it.

I thought, "This looks like the ultimate scene of an action movie combining Bruce Willis and Arnold Schwarzenegger together." The devastation was immense!

I walked out to West Street to see the activity by the command post. I noticed a fire engine still idling on the corner of West Street and Chambers Street. I do not remember the number on the truck or what borough it was from. I just remember the unnatural sight of the dust on the inside of the windshield, the dust on the jump seats were the firemen sat. I could see a light jacket a fireman had been wearing left on the jump seat; it too was covered with a layer of dust, now deeper than yesterday.

As the time passed, hours seemed like minutes as the lives of people disappeared in smoky wisps. It's hard to recall everything now since my memory of these horrific scenes is blurry.

VI

The Longest Day in EMS History.
Wednesday September 12, 2001

*The city is going to survive, we are going to get through it.
It's going to be very, very difficult time. I don't think we yet
know the pain that we're going to feel when we find out who
we lost, but the thing we have to focus on now is getting this
city through this, and surviving and being stronger for it.*
— *Mayor Rudolph Giuliani*

My body was tight from walking all night and carrying the backpack. As the sun rose slowly, streaks of light traced over the buildings around the World Trade Center wreckage. The light was like healing hands feeling the scorched skin of a patient.

As morning dawned the chatter of jackhammers started slowly. Soon the noise could be heard everywhere. With the sun rise, chatter of jackhammers and other machinery, the realization was setting in that this was our reality, not some nightmare or bad dream from eating too much chili and going to bed late. This was really happening and now there was no denying it.

We started our day by forming teams and assembling those who were to be assigned with fire search companies. We were told to meet them at 08:00. However, the fire teams went out at 07:00 and apparently did not want any outsiders with them. The fire department had lost hundreds of men and it was important to them that they recover their men, without any help, on their own. I'd like to think it would be handy to have 2 USAR medics to treat the patient if they found one of their brothers alive or if they were injured.

So, we went in pairs of two walking around and looking for trapped people in the rubble. We walked down Church Street and saw the façade of Number Seven World Trade Center on the street. A ladder company was still spraying water on the wreckage to suppress a lingering smoky fire.

We walked to the opening between Number Four and Number Five World Trade Center. The scene was an awesome sight. The two buildings were scorched and burned out with major damage from falling debris from the Twin Towers.

**Ladder Company Spraying Water on the Wreckage of
7 World Trade Center
(Photo courtesy of Bobby Wong)**

I thought, "I can't imagine what it must have been like to be here when the Towers came rumbling and falling down with debris the size of houses falling on the street and those below." We walked between the buildings and looked out over the pit, a vast wasteland of twisted metal and debris. Again, I wondered, "How can anyone survive this mess?"

There was a long piece of steel hanging and moving slightly. You could see debris for thousands of feet off the concrete walkway. It reminded me of going to the dump with my father when I was a kid. We would drive trash to the dump, walk out to the edge and through our trash into the pile.

This pile was different though. As I walked I was aware that there were victims beneath us, in some cases co-workers, brothers in arms who were missing and probably long dead.

As we ventured out to the area where rescue operations where in progress I was aware of the feeling that my feet where walking on a pile of debris where hundreds maybe thousands of people where lost. I saw a police officer's hat in one spot, a PD tactical baton in another spot, a firemen's helmet, and a Halligan tool in the pile (This tool is used to force doors open at house fires).

To see these items without their owners was startling. Each of these items defined the person who was wearing them. You would never see any of these items left anywhere, not in the street, not in the open. When I looked at the Halligan tool, I remembered the face of the last fireman I saw use one of those. "There you go EMS, she's open now," the fireman said to me after using it.

Next, I heard bullets discharging in the area of the fire. This is when I was reminded once again that I was walking on debris that contained bodies.

I thought, "This shit is off the hook!"

Wanting to do something productive, I joined the line of people who were passing debris away from the rescue area out to the street for disposal. The line was efficient. An object for a bucket of debris would come down the line and be passed right to the person next in line. I started to help lift metal, but then realized I could get cut. I reverted to standby, but still I had feeling that I should be doing something.

I saw some construction workers between number Four and Five

WTC and asked, "What are you doing here? Were you working on a job?"

One of the guys told me, "No, our fathers and grandfathers built this building, we are here to help. This building is family to us. Our unions called us up and told us to come down and help rescue people, we know how to cut and move steel. This is what we do."

I replied, "Wow! I respect your dedication."

Since there were many people left to pass debris I realized I had better not get injured moving it, especially when we were supposed to be treating patients. I kept walking and looked out over the wreckage. All I see is a bunch of I-beams and waste. I wondered, "Where are the victims? Are they in some void somewhere or are they all gone?"

My thought was interrupted by the call from across the area, "Medic. Medic."

I was being called to go out in the pile where people had been found. This was a hit; time to go to work. I walked step-by-step in the narrow path that the line had cleared. At points I was on a narrow I-beam balancing the pack and all.

"Here, give me your pack," an ironworker said.

I handed him the backpack and down the line it went.

I thought, "God, I hope I get that back."

As I now walked more comfortably I got support on both side from the people in the line. At some points I was barely touching the ground as I was gently lifted 6 to 8 inches at a time with hands supporting me from all sides. I briskly covered the 80 feet or so to the site where there were patients. As I reached the excavation site I looked for my equipment. I saw my pack at the front of the line.

Bystanders were waving for me to come over, not a frantic wave, but a calm "over here" wave.

When we respond to a cardiac arrest we know it is a real job because there is usually someone out front in a t-shirt or nightie waving frantically with both arms, "over here, over here." We call it the cardiac arrest wave. This was not the same urgency.

I thought, "This can't be good."

"Down there," the construction worker said, "I'll hold the pack. I don't think you'll need any equipment."

I wondered what awaited me. I thought of the details the USAR medics had told us about the 1995 Oklahoma City bombing of the Murrah Federal Building becoming a recovery zone. I was sure this was going to be bad. As I shuffled across a large concrete slab I saw a void, a huge void. Shuffling along I had my light in front of me and, soon enough, I saw four bodies that were pinned under the concrete wreckage.

I pronounced, "Dead, dead, dead and dead." There was nothing to be done for these people. These were not patients; they were fatalities.

I looked over the bodies and saw a clothes shop of some kind. This must have been the basement of the Trade Center. The clothes were on a rack and the counter was intact. It looked like you could have turned on the power and sold dresses. I envisioned the woman talking to a customer about a good business dress for her future big meeting as a sales pitch.

The people seemed to be just frozen in time in one horrible moment. This must be a corridor that fell over on top of the store. I began to realize that I was not sure how stable this mess was, so I needed to get out and call this in.

"Maybe we can work here and get these people out," I thought.

I called in to the USAR base, gave a location and number of bodies. I was exhilarated that I had found some bodies, but I was greeted with a flat "Ok, and we will let the proper authorities know."

That is the kind of smack down a dispatcher gives you when you ask for something stupid or impossible. This was his kind of way of saying, "Yeah, right." As I heard this I realized this was a huge mess and I should not have called in the location. There was nothing that can be done. Bodies will be removed when the area is cleaned; voids and the living come first.

I looked around and for 360 degrees around me was apocalyptic damage to the buildings; there was total annihilation and no sign of anyone alive. Here there was absence of life or hope; it was a cold dank, void of activity. The bodies of these people would have to wait due course; their discovery was incidental.

I climbed back out and began to walk toward the next area where rescuers were working. We spent the morning standing by and looking over the remains of victims who were found, the description of which should only be left in the mind of rescuers who had to see them.

I made my way out to West Street and was relieved to be walking on pavement, dust and dirt covered albeit, but flat pavement. I saw a familiar face approaching me, I could not place who it was. The NYPD Uniform with eagle collar brass threw me off. It looked like it was Dr. Martinez in a dress NYPD uniform.

I said, "Good morning sir. How are you doing? What is with the uniform?"

He replied, "I am a PD surgeon, assimilated rank of Deputy Chief."

I quipped, "I guess you never got over that ticket you got in your jeep?"

He looked and took a double take and said, "You remember that?"

"Yes I do Doc, that was a great story."

As I continue on, I see Chief Friedman. "Hey Chief."

"Lt. Kanarian, how are you?"

"Good sir and you?"

"I am a bit overwhelmed. I have enjoyed seeing some familiar faces and all but this is a terrible day. I am overwhelmed with the complements from people I have not seen in years. Steve, this is a terrible tragedy but it is nice to see people I have not seen in years. Medics who are now cops and fire captains thanked me for the way I treated them. I was really just doing the right thing, you know?"

I replied, "Yeah, I know Chief. Unfortunately we have a lot of bosses who don't care about people."

"Days like this should be a wake up call for everybody," he said.

I gave Chief Freidman a hug and moved on. "Boy he is the best," I thought.

In the midst of this disaster, in which thousands of people were lost, rescuers from different parts of the city renewed old acquaintances and were relieved to find another rescuer they know alive.

Evening Duty

Our team Captain spoke. He told us we would be rotating with the NYPD ESU (Emergency Services Unit), which is the tactical arm of the police department for rescue and tactical operations. USAR component, 2 medics per team, 12-hour shifts; and we were to follow the direction of the team leader.

"Cool, now we are getting organized," I thought, nodding my head.

We were standing against the wall on West Street looking around at the scene the wreckage was unfathomable and there were no landmarks to use to begin to recognize features of the World Trade Center. One of the USAR team members kept saying, "If I can see the ball I can find my way around." However, the gold globe of the Word Trade Center was still not visible. Later, we saw the remnants of the shattered gold globe in the wreckage.

Remnants of the Shattered Gold Globe in the Wreckage

As I looked around the site I noticed an EMS turnout coat in the dirt. I picked it up and put it on the wall. Next, I saw an oxygen regulator on the ground with an oxygen tank. Suddenly, I began to see equipment everywhere. There was a pile of long boards, suction containers and ambulance equipment that had been taken off of destroyed ambulances. These items were one-for-one items that EMTs and paramedics are personally responsible for. Things you do not just leave around.

I thought, "For this many one-for-one items to be left on the ground there must have been Hell going on around them."

The sergeant went to go talk to the FDNY SOC chief at the entrance of the parking garage. Our mission that night was to try to get into the basement and gain access to the area where the deli was. Supposedly there were reports of a police officer and 10 civilians who were trapped down below. As I looked over to where the ESU sergeant was talking to the Fire Chief I also saw a Port Authority ranking officer talking.

I could not hear the conversation but I could see the head of the SOC chief. He is an experienced and weathered chief, a chief who has seen many things I am sure. His helmet is melted in places and has been weathered slowly with years of experience. I could see that he was rising to the occasion and getting the job done.

As the ESU sergeant talked and pointed toward the entry to the parking garage, the SOC Chief was turning his head indicating *No.* He then turned to the opening and explained why they wouldn't go down there. The ESU sergeant was talking and using his charming Irish personality and inspiration to get the job done. Slowly I noticed the SOC chief's body language change and he gave a reluctant head turn to the side and a nod to agree to a plan. They each nodded their heads and the SOC chief turned and agreed to the plan.

I thought, "Wow! If the Sergeant can get this done, anything is possible."

It was nice to see the three agencies pulling in one direction. I felt that anything was possible now with everybody working together.

A little while later, the ESU Sergeant returned and gave the thumbs up sign. "Ok, they are going to go down there with two of us. FDNY is reluctant to go down there because they lost guys down there. They agreed to go down and check it out to see if we can access the lower levels."

The donned Scott Air Paks. The Sergeant and an ESU officer went down into the parking lot with the FDNY SOC Chief and a team of Port Authority Officers. We settled back to lean on the low wall and looked around at the scene.

I thought, "Incredible, what must have transpired here is unimaginable."

A cold, driving rain began to fall on us and I used the found turnout coat to cover my legs. I don't mind being chilled, but I did not want to get wet and chilled because conduction of heat through water is the most efficient form of heat loss. I checked my watch and noticed that five minutes had passed.

Later on, I saw a familiar face. I didn't recognize him immediately but it appeared to be someone I know. His name came to me, "It's John McCullough."

I greeted him saying, "Hi John, how are you?"

He replied, "Good Steve, how are you doing?"

I remarked, "Good, quite a day, isn't it?"

John said, "Yes it is. I can't believe that the sergeant got FDNY SOC Chief to agree to go down into the parking lot. He is an amazing boss."

I know John from upstate New York. We worked per diem for a paramedic agency there and then he became an ESU Officer. John was assigned to Truck Four in the Bronx. It was nice to see a friendly face on a night like this.

"Good to see you Steve, take care," John said.

After twenty minutes the team emerged from the parking garage and the ESU Sergeant took off his mask. Shaking his head the Sergeant said, "When they said they lost guys down there, I thought it was five or six guys; they have seven two-and-a-half inch hoses that go off the edge into the abyss. Each hose had four or five guys on it. The garage entry is no use; carbon monoxide (CO) levels are through the roof. The CO meter sounded as we entered the garage, the doors that lead into the trade center are racked and unable to be opened. We will have to try another way, perhaps from the subway side."

Number 5 World Trade Center

The ESU sergeant said, "Well guys lets get going; we will head over to 5 World Trade Center and see if we can gain access from there. I hate to have you guys carry this stuff over but there is no alternative. I tried to get a Gator utility vehicle from that EMS chief but she would not give it up. It would be great to have it for an hour or so just to get our equipment over this debris."

I stepped slowly looking down and checking each spot where I put my foot; the metal was sharp and angular. Metal is not like rock. If you are walking on rock there is something for your boot to grab hold of. Metal is smooth and very slippery, especially when covered with dust. I fixed my respirator mask and stepped cautiously. I thought, "Next event like this I bet ESU has dozens of their own Gators."

We progressed very slowly through the pit area over the debris and toward Number 5 World Trade Center. We walked past a line of firefighters who were digging with hand tools and putting debris and dirt into buckets to remove them from the search area. The buckets were then passed down the line and dumped. It did not seem possible to conduct an excavation with buckets, but they were determined and steadfast.

We reached the outside perimeter of the pit and stepped into the street. The roadway was clear and easy to walk on. We continued on to Chambers Street to Number Five World Trade Center. Walking down the steps we see the tile floors and the nice décor of the building. The atrium is markedly devoid of people.

I thought, "This building was always filled with people and teeming with activity all day long. There always were business people leaving the subway to make important presentations and deals in the World Trade Center. People were usually playing instruments in the subway entrance; they were all gone." The building was quiet.

We walked down the steps to the promenade level and saw the dark catacomb-like hallway. On the right I saw a jewelry store with the gate opened slightly. Peering in from the entryway I saw no people, no victims. The shelves were stocked and papers were on the counter, but life was interrupted. The next store was a magazine store that was open. The store was fully stocked with candies, soda and magazines.

I looked down on the counter and there was the *New York Times* September 11, 2001 newspaper. Looking at the paper, I surmised,

"Wow! Life will be different from now on. This is the last newspaper before the collapse of the Twin Towers."

The ESU Lieutenant advised us to not touch anything except the water. He said we could take the water and drink what we wanted.

We moved down the hallway and saw darkness and empty hallways. As we approached a store entry I saw markings from a USAR team who had searched the area. This meant that the area has already been searched and there was nothing here for us to do. I heard movement to my left. As I turned my light to the left I got a fleeting view of two rats fleeing the beam of light.

I thought, "There is nobody down here. Nobody for us to help."

Number 4 World Trade Center

As we moved indoors down into Number 4 World Trade Center I saw a watch store full of contents and a deli. We confiscated water and nothing else. I did not think to take a newspaper that reported the last signs of normal life here right there on the counter. We drank the warm water and moved along.

The USAR markings were found near the stores as we walked down the corridors. A rat or two were seen as we put lights into the shadows. The building looked dead and vacant, like a body without a soul.

As we worked I looked up and saw an unusual sight. I noticed in the shadows of the building the American Flag was hanging on the face of the World Financial Center. The flag struck me funny in that the flag was being displayed to represent the country, not as a matter of routine.

I had been to many serious jobs and mass casualty incidents but had never seen the American Flag hung at a job.

I thought, "This job is different." I knew I would never be the same.

Operations ceased around 3:30 am. We headed back to the base camp where we took off our packs, washed our boots in the boot wash, and washed our faces with cold water from water bottles. It felt good to take the respirator mask off and get clean. "This is bullshit,"

I thought, "I need a good shower and a change of underwear." I sat down for a while and rested. "God, I could use a cup of tea!"

I was aggravated by the fiberglass particles irritating my neck and back. I had not changed clothes in 3 days, I was wearing the same clothes in which I was doing heavy work and had exposure to grime.

"Enough!" I thought. I walked to the "General Store" and got some fresh socks and clean underwear. I then walked back to the base camp and looked for a shower. A soldier who was assembling generators told me the shower was in the Community College in the gym.

"Awesome," I thanked him.

"Hey, brother, by the way, there is no heat in lower Manhattan, it will be a cold shower," the soldier told me.

"That's fine with me." I proceeded toward the Community College of Manhattan and headed for the gym. NYPD had established a staging area in the gym and had desks, chairs and cots available for police officers.

An officer asked me, "Can I help you L-T?"

"Yes, I am looking for the showers."

"They are on your left through the men's locker room; watch out though there is no hot water. Really, L-T, it is very cold."

"Thank you." I said as I walked with determination to the men's locker room. I would not be dissuaded from taking a shower.

My friend Kevin had always said I would not survive the post-nuclear world because I had a waterbed and liked the good life.

I thought, "Wish he could see me now. I am doing pretty well. I don't know how many more days I can work straight out, but I am good for now."

I took a cold shower and was happy to rinse off. Cold was an understatement! This water was freezing and felt like razor blades as it hit my skin, but I needed to get clean and get some measure of dignity back. As I washed I could see the black grime in the water collecting on the floor.

I thought, "Wow, this is nasty shit! Feel better already." I figured, "I am not comfortable nor is it healthy to have God knows what on my skin." I thought, "Kevin, I am doing alright. This is as close as I will come to the post-nuclear world, I hope, and I am doing well."

I threw out my underwear and put on some foot powder and new socks.

I thought, "Wow, it felt like Christmas morning!"

I had to wear the same old uniform because they were not letting unidentified personnel down to Ground Zero. My uniform was stiff from the dust and crap that had accumulated in spots not covered by the backpack.

VII
Homeward Bound.
Thursday September 13, 2001

Morning, Heading Home

We had a 09:00 briefing with the team medical director. He addressed all of us saying, "Gentlemen, you have done a superb job rising to the challenge all the way. We are obviously going to be here a long time. We are going to break the team up into shifts and rotate in twelve hour shifts for the duration. Check the roster for your assignments. Some of you will stay on today for the day shift, others will get to go home and come back tonight at 19:00. Don't get too comfortable at home. You have to get your butts back here tonight. Report to the Academy at 18:00 hours. That is all."

Since we were dismissed, we piled into the truck and waited for the rest of the team members.

I thought, "Let's go brother, we want to go home!"

We drove back to the Academy and were stopped at the gate and asked to show our ID by MPs at the gate.

We tell the MP "My God man, can't you see we have been downtown for two days in a row?"

An MP said, "Sorry sirs, we need to see some ID."

We looked around in disbelief. Here we were in a department vehicle wearing uniforms covered in dust from Ground Zero and they wanted to see our IDs. They peered in the back and waved us on into the Academy grounds.

I found my car and started the drive home.

I headed over to the station to get the rest of my uniforms and submit my time sheet. In my Toyota Corolla I enjoyed the feel of the soft seat. It was not a luxury car but it was something other than metal or a metal seat or the hard ground. I drove home carefully realizing I had been working straight out for forty-eight hours.

I opened the window and enjoyed the fresh air. On the radio, stations played songs that had been modified with 9/11 sound bytes over them. During the drive home I felt drained and vacant. I remember driving along the highway and remarking how washed out everything looked. The world was grey, the sky, the Hudson River, the superstructure of the bridge the cars in front of me — everything was grey.

As I drove across the George Washington Bridge, I noticed the steel supports and how they were properly secured with large rivets and not burned and twisted. A tractor-trailer passed by me and I clearly remember seeing the Bulldog on the front of the truck leaning forward on its two hind legs as if to say, "We are still working and still running the country, in your face pal!"

As the truck passed I saw a huge American Flag on the bulkhead of the truck. The American Flag waved in the wind proudly as the truck drove. I noticed the bright red, white, and blue of the flag. The flag alone looked like the only thing in the world that had color. I noticed the crisp borders between the stripes and the brilliant white stars on a field of blue.

I was reminded that each star represented a State and all of its people, people who had pulled together and fought for freedom.

I thought, "People coming together is what makes this great country."

Whether is was farmers picking up rifles in the revolutionary war or the rescuers filling buckets on their hands and knees at the World Trade Center collapse, we all come together as one. I will never forget that feeling of seeing the bright colors of the flag on the truck that read "Brooklyn Lumber Yard" pulling the trailer that held that huge flag as I drove home. That sight gave me goose bumps and the energy to drive home.

Gratefully, I made it home. I knew that this uniform did not belong in my home. I went into the garage and undressed, placed my uniform in a bag and took a long hot shower. I showered in my own bathroom, gave my kids a hug and kissed my wife. All I wanted to do was to go to bed, my bed, in my home.

My wife told the kids to "let your father sleep. He is tired."

I was aware of their soft touch and sweet smell, but I was very tired and just needed to sleep. I went to bed and slept.

I woke up in what seemed like an instant, but it was 3:00 pm. I heated the water and made a large cup of tea. I went and sat in the front of my house and put my feet up in the sun. The afternoon sun felt good on my face. I aired out my feet and looked at the blisters and red marks from pressure.

I thought, "Feet don't fail me now, we have more work to do."

I continued to air out my feet, sit and relax as the sun and air dried the moist skin and helped heal the blisters from walking and climbing on uneven metal surfaces.

I drank my tea and looked at the American flag flying high in my neighbors yard. My neighbor was a career Navy man who flew the flag every day on a white pole that stands forty feet in the air. His house was adorned with Navy pictures and emblems around on his walls. He even had "NAVY" vanity license plate.

Looking next door to the Navy house I saw they also had the American Flag hanging in front of their house. I looked to my right and my neighbors also had the American flag up. As I looked around I noticed that all the houses on my block had the American Flag flying in front of their houses.

I walked across my grass in my bare feet and peered around the corner, down the block. Every single house had the American flag up. I had never seen such a display of patriotism, even on the Fourth of July.

"Wow!" I thought "What a thing for everybody to be united and pulling in the same direction. There was not one exception."

I took advantage of being home to think, while in a safe place to sit. A flood of thoughts came through my mind. Tears wanted to flow but the well was dry.

I remembered my Grandfather's funeral the month before in Rhode Island. My grandfather died from cancer of the larynx; he had his larynx removed some eight years before. Earlier in the summer he had a reoccurrence of cancer and was unable to escape the spread of cancer through his body. A lifetime of smoking unfiltered cigarettes had caught up with him.

On holidays our relatives would smoke Chesterfields and the apartment would fill with a familiar stench. The kids would play pool and hide and seek in the cool basement.

I recalled that as I stood next to his coffin in the memorial chapter I looked at his lifeless body and thought of all the great things he had done for us. He would take us shopping on the weekend and let us buy models and trains. I bought an American LaFrance Ladder truck and completed it with pride, bright red and white.

When my Grandfather was lowered into the ground I was deep in thought of the Saturday nights we sat and would watch The Lawrence Welk Show and then Emergency! My Grandfather always respected the "Fire Teams." On Christmas and holidays we would listen to the scanner and hear the firemen dispatched to emergencies: Rescue 1 Difficulty and breathing. Engine 2 respond Water flooding a house," and other routine business of the fire department.

Occasionally the rescue and fire truck would race by his apartment and make the building shiver. "There go the fire teams, they know what to do," he would say with great respect.

"Ba-Blaam! Ba-Blaam, Ba-Blaam!" My thoughts were interrupted by a report of rifles that echoed in my chest. Retired military personnel fired a six-gun salute for my Grandfather.

I was startled and knew his death was final. I asked one of the soldiers "Why a six gun salute?" The soldier told me, "Your grandfather served in the Navy during World War II, but he was Stateside."

I remember thinking, "My grandfather, my father, and my uncles all served our country in war. I will never have served my country."

I know my Grandfather was very proud of me being a paramedic in New York City, but in the end I thought that I would have never served my country.

Now as I looked around the neighborhood looking at the Americana flags rustling gently in the September breeze, recalling the American Flag I saw at Ground Zero, I realized, I am no longer working just for New York City, we are serving our country now.

I popped up and got ready to go back downtown. Tonight I am using powder and wearing two pairs of socks, and bringing extras.

Bob Reeg

While I was getting ready for work, my wife interrupted me and said, "I want to tell you some news. Good news, mostly."

"What is wrong?" I asked while wondering, "What is about to be dropped on me now?"

Moira replied, "Marie Reeg called. Bob was injured in the collapse of the World Trade Center."

I dropped my head and waited for the news.

She continued, "He will be ok. He has a chest injury and blood in his lung."

"Oh, a hemothorax," I answered.

"Yeah, that is what she said. He is going home in two days."

"I exhaled a sigh of relief. I was glad Bob was going to be ok.

As I left to return to Ground Zero, Moira exclaimed, "Stay safe down there!"

I replied, "Will do. Love you, Bye."

As I drove downtown, I thought about Bob Reeg and wondered what could have happened to him. Bob was a firefighter in Engine Company 44, uptown. Given the large loss of life in the FDNY, I was grateful Bob was ok.

I recalled that Moira and I met Bob and Marie at a Saint Patrick's Day corned beef and cabbage dinner at church. I was trying to avoid telling him I worked for EMS after I found out he was a FNDY firefighter because we met in 1997 when the nerves where still raw on both sides of the merger. My wife urged me to tell him, so I announced, "I too work for FDNY. I am an EMS lieutenant and paramedic."

Bob's response was far different than I expected. He replied, "I too worked for EMS. I was a medic at Jacobi. You know some of my partners, Chief McKracken, Chief Ianarelli, Jimmy Lombardi and all the rest."

"Really, what was EMS like back then?" I inquired.

He replied, "It was crazy. We used to turn ambulances over regularly; sometimes we turned them over end-to end."

Little did I know this quintessential Irishman in a rope sweater at a church dinner with his wife and kids would become a good friend through the years. We became good friends through a shared common experience of being paramedics.

Later when I had a chance to talk to Bob about what happened on 9/11, he told me, "My company responded to the Twin Towers on the second 5th alarm. I knew this was bad. This was intentional, two planes just don't hit the Towers. This was terrorism. I knew fifty-thousand people were going to die that day."

Bob continued, "We were in staging to go into the Tower where chiefs were sending companies in one after another. By some twist of fate, a chief put his hand up and told us to stop. Then he asked, What company are you? I answered Engine 44, Sir? He said, "Good! Put these car fires out and keep West Street open. I moved out of line with my company and the other companies were sent into the Towers, in, in, inside. As we went to the engine to get our equipment, I pushed up the cabinet door and saw the Towers starting to collapse. I yelled, *Run, Run for your lives, Lads, She is coming down.*"

He explained, "As my company ran, I was blown through the air. When I landed, I had severe chest pain and shortness of breath; I was coughing up dust and debris. I was able to feel my way through the dust to an idling police van that had the air conditioning on. I climbed inside and passed out. When I regained consciousness I was being helped to an ambulance by two police officers. I knew they were ESU cops because of the distinctive holsters ESU cops wear to protect their weapons from violent emotionally disturbed people. I never saw their faces. I was taken by ambulance to Saint Vincent's Hospital in Manhattan."

I thought, "The world sure works in mysterious ways. I am glad Bob is ok."

Night, Returning to Ground Zero

Soon it was time to head back to work; we had to be at the Academy by 18:00 hours so we could get to Ground Zero to relieve the day team at 19:00 hours. Driving over the bridge I started questioning myself about returning to the collapse site.

"What if something happens? Should I really be going back down there? What about my family? Should I not be staying home?"

As I thought about the risk of going downtown, I realized we had a duty to get back downtown and do our job. I reassured myself, "Everything will be fine. We have a lot of work to do."

I thought clearly about going downtown, I consciously said I will see my family tomorrow; it was time to go to work. I felt the personal part of my life being secured in a safe place in the back of my mind; I was now able to focus on the task at hand.

I looked to my right and saw the smoke from Ground Zero and thought "Why can't they get a grip on that fire? The fire must be really down deep to be burning this long."

My mind wandered to thoughts of the victims in the rubble, and how as a fire burns it generates smoke, heat, and carbon monoxide. I thought, "These victims have been through enough; now they were being subjected to the heat and deadly gases."

I thought about our training and how carbon monoxide is 220 times more attracted to hemoglobin than oxygen. I also thought about the heat and lack of oxygen. I realized that the odds of someone surviving this long where very grim.

At the Academy, we were told there might not be a truck available to bring us downtown. I could not believe the attitude of the lieutenant who said, "We have an Academy to run you know. This truck should be assigned to us going back and forth."

Finally they agreed to let us use the truck as long as their driver drove so they knew they would get the truck back.

"This was absurd," I thought.

We piled into an old Chevy Suburban. There were not enough seats, so a couple of us jumped in the rear area. I was filled with energy as we drove through the streets towards Ground Zero. Next we saw passersby waving and holding signs that said "Thank You

Rescuers." Wow, what a feeling to have the support of the public on such a big job. Normally we get attitude from New Yorkers as our ambulances are usually blocking the street or just somehow annoying people. Today, the country was all on the same page.

Passersby Waving and Thanking Rescuers
(Photo Courtesy of FEMA/Andrea Booher)

Heading down West Street we saw people waiving and thanking us for our work. I stopped and thought, "What work are they talking about? We have done a lot of waiting and looking not much rescuing." Then I realized "The fact that someone was trying to do something in a time when the average person cannot begin to know what to do was enough for the public. Perhaps all we were doing is preserving a wisp of hope."

The day crew was glad to see us, and Roger remarked, "Shit, I am surprised you fairies came back."

"Hey, how is it going Jay?" I said.

"Good," he replied.

Another teammate spurted, "Hey we met some stars today. VIP's were everywhere."

Ralph and Gerry grinned and commented, pointing to each other, "We met DeNiro."

"Get out!" I replied, "Really?"

Ralph said, "Yeah. We were walking back from the pit and we

saw a crowd around Robert DeNiro. He was surrounded by civilians, shaking hands and signing autographs. We did not have the energy to fight to the middle so we watched. When he saw us he stopped what he was doing and came out of the crowd to thank us. He gave us a big hug."

We reported to the base camp and got our equipment ready for the night tour. I noticed some equipment had been appropriated and was used by the day tour. I emptied my back of the frills we did not need. I carried just the basics.

I thought, "Tonight would be a good night to find some patients trapped, the rescuers are digging in deeper and the weather has been good. Maybe tonight we will get somebody out."

We walked to the ESU base and met up with the teams we had been going out with. Mike took us over to the equipment tent and showed us around. They had some nice newer helmets and flashlights, good equipment to have on a job like this. As we traveled with the ESU Officers in the stake body truck, we noticed that now the streets were somewhat clear around the periphery of the site. We were able to drive a few blocks. Then National Guardsmen in combat fatigues carrying weapons stopped us.

"I need to see your IDs and passes," the guard said.

One of the ESU officers replied, "What did he say? Open the damn gate, we are NYPD."

"I need to see your IDs and passes," the guard reiterated.

It would be one thing to be on a truck with construction workers or volunteers, but here was a truck with sixteen ESU Officers who were all business — rock and roll types, the top of the food chain in NYPD. NYPD has a saying, when the public needs help they call 911, when a cop needs help they call ESU. These guys have unquestionable integrity and are never refused access anywhere.

An ESU officer stood up and yelled out, "Open the gate, this is our city!"

The soldier looked up at him and a second soldier and repeated, "I need to see your IDs and passes."

Apparently in the 12 hours we had been off there had been a fence put up around Ground Zero and the National Guard was securing the Broadway and Church Street entrances.

The officer who stood up pointed to his NYPD patch and yelled, "This is my ID, and this is my pass, as he grasped his weapon. Open the gate now!"

The weapon was squarely secured in a protected leather holster, but easily accessible if needed. An officer from the National Guard came over and talked with the NYPD Lieutenant in the front seat. The gate was quickly opened and we drove through.

ESU Police Officers Attempting to Cut I-Beams

We moved to the middle of West Street and set up a workspace. Our job was to stand by and wait for victims to be located and to look after injured team members. The ESU police officers had gotten a hold of a special steel cutting torch to cut the I-beams. They were somewhat enthusiastic about the prospect of cutting the steel and making some progress toward finding voids to search.

Slowly the ESU officers cut the beam and worked away. Hours passed and the officers tried different approaches to the metal, different angles. Some cuts were made but progress was slow. Looking around the site on West Street the blue smoke and mountains of metal debris made me think of Hell itself. This was an eerie place and there were no indications of life; no reason to have hope.

Over in the distance another crew was cutting with an acetylene torch. You could see the smoke rising above the hole they had cleared in the debris, all solid steel I-beams.

"They should watch out for fumes," I commented to Lou Matallana.

He replied, "No we are outside Steve. It should not be a problem."

I thought, "You never know, the fumes could be heavier than air."

ESU Officers Attempting to Cut the I-Beams

I looked to my right and then to my left. As far as the eye could see long lines of rescuers and construction workers stretched across the pile from the edge deep into the pile. Bucket by bucket, piece-by-piece the debris was sent from the middle to the perimeter of the pile.

I heard a yell, "*Run.*"

I saw men diving out of the hole they had been clearing in the pile. A couple of the men dove over the pile into sheer metal. I heard a Whoooosh sound! A bright blue flame filled the air above the hole they were working in. A fire had started. A fireman put an extinguisher over the hole, sprayed a couple of times and then peered over the top.

"OK, all clear," the fireman yelled, and then everyone went back to work.

American Flag Flying in the Pit

Among the I-beams, I had found a comfortable spot where the backpack cushioned my back from the metal and my feet rested in a pile of metal shavings and cement dust that actually felt like dirt. My feet felt a little relaxed.

The line of volunteers went from the site we were digging around into an arch over some debris pile and then out to the front of the World Financial Center. I would watch as buckets would go from hand-to-hand through the site to the edge where it was dumped, then a couple of buckets would be piled together and sent back out to the pile for filling. We were looking at a site of about 16 acres of land that was filled with wreckage that was beyond any average person's imagination, or the rescuers' imagination for that matter.

I saw a man down in the hole look up and ask for some water. The Captain turned to the line and shouted, "Send us water!"

Down the line the message went: "water, water, water," around the bend, over the debris pile and back to the edge. In seconds two cases of water bottles were coming out and down the line around the bend and over the debris pile.

Line of Volunteers Passing Equipment and Supplies in the Pit

I said to my partner Lou, "Did you see that? That was awesome."

Another order was given, "Shovels, shovels, shovels." A package of ten shovels wrapped in plastic came down the line.

"Amazing," I thought. I leaned forward to the line and called out "food, we need food."

Down the line the message went "Food, food, food." A box was sent down the line consisting of Red Cross sandwiches and small bags of chips.

"Watch this, Lou." I shouted out "$50,000 dollars, we need money" to the line.

"Yo, brother, you are too tired. Get some rest. That one ain't happening," someone shouted back.

We all laughed. I did this to release the stress and tension that had built up because of our inability to find people. Slowly the routine continued in the line, buckets went out, they were condensed and then sent back out to the pile.

Chicago FD Chief

As Lou and I were standing on West Street watching the rescue scene in front of us I heard some rustling of the metal and debris below us to the left. I saw a piece of metal get pushed upright and then fall backward, dust jumped into the air and I saw movement below the dust.

"What the Hell is this?" I wondered.

I looked over and could see the tip of a pike pole and firefighters helmet light tying to pierce the dust in the rubble below. I walked over to the I-beam nearest this recent activity and saw two firemen in the hole. I saw a flashlight beam point around and a voice asked, "Brother, could you pull the pike pole, give us a lift?"

As I pulled on the pike pole a firefighter emerged from the depths of debris. I was surprised to see the helmet shield, which read, "Chicago FD Chief."

As I pulled him up I greeted him, "Hello Chief, how are you?"

Another fireman came up out of the hole behind the Chief. We pulled him up as he traversed the smooth metal surface of the I pillar.

I asked them, "What are you guys doing here?"

"Oh, if we don't belong here, let us know we will leave," the Chief replied.

"I mean it is OK for you to be here, Chicago is one of the big ten fire departments in the country. I was just wondering did you guys tunnel over, or take the train."

We all laughed a little.

The Fire Chief replied, "We saw the Twin Towers collapse and we had to come and help our brothers. We did not know where we would sleep or eat; we just knew we had to be here. We planned to drive out after our shift and get to work. A local RV dealer gave us a mobile home to use for free; we have a vehicle to drive and a place to stay while we are here."

"Welcome Chief." We are glad to have your help, I said.

We stood and looked at the two Chicago Firefighters as they looked around. I thought about the accounts I had read of the Great Chicago Fire and how New York City and Boston had sent fire trucks on rail cars during the Great Chicago Fire, which allegedly was started by Mrs. O'Leary's cow.

I said, "Chief, I guess this is a lot like the Great Chicago fire."

He looked at me and replied, "Lou, this is a lot worse than the Great Chicago Fire."

We all nodded in agreement. I guessed he was right. This was worse. What a sensation to be working on a job compared with a historical event like the Great Chicago Fire and then to dwarf that event. I am not sure if any firefighters were lost during the Great Chicago Fire and yet here we are looking for hundreds of rescuers, EMS, firefighters and policemen, and thousands of civilians.

I thought about the great fires and disasters I had read about growing up — The Iroquois Theatre fire in Chicago and the Coconut Grove Supper Club fire. I had responded to the Happy Land fire, which was the biggest homicide in US history, at least until September 11th.

The comparison was staggering to me. I had grown up wanting to be a firefighter, reading about the great fires and disasters in US history. Now I am standing in the wreckage of the worst disaster in US history. I thought about how it was to be here looking around in amazement. I never thought I would be at such a big historical event.

The Rescue Dog with Hypothermia

Lou and I were standing against an I-beam, and I was enjoying a soft spot of dust and metal shavings that felt like earth. The steel and debris was so hard my feet hurt pretty badly after continuously walking and standing on steel. I had found a spot that was soft on my feet and from where I could watch the rescuers dig.

A female police officer made eye contact with me and then another officer motioned for us to come over. They were waving for us to come over to their location, which was about 50 steps away, fifty steps on angular metal and steel. I got up and adjusted my pack. Lou and I walked over to their location.

"What's up?" I asked.

One officer replied, "Our dog is shivering, no matter how many blankets we put over the dog he is shivering." The officers had removed their coats to put over the dog to no avail. Lou lifted up the coats and blankets to examine the dog. We looked at the dog that was lying on a large sheet of metal.

Lou asked the officer, "Can you pick up the dog?"

The officer picked up the 150-pound German shepherd who was obviously hypothermic and shivering out of control. I placed two blankets under the dog and they lowered it onto the blankets. We covered the dog and petted the dog's head. Within a few minutes the dog stopped shivering.

The officer asked, "What was wrong?"

I replied, "The metal sheet was absorbing all of the heat from the dog. The blankets on top were keeping heat in, but underneath your dog's heat was being absorbed by the steel beam. Metal acts like a heat sink and will drain a person or a dog of all their heat in time, at least down to the outside temperature."

"Thank you so much, I never would have thought of that," the officer replied.

I said, "That is one of the first things we do for patients trapped in a collapsed building."

"Thanks Brother."

"Not a problem."

I looked back and tried to figure out where the soft spot we had found was. So much had changed in the last ten minutes, people had shifted, the line had moved. Where was that spot. We decided it was easier to stay with the officers and the dog. At least we were able to help the dog, our first patient.

VIII
Night at Ground Zero.
Friday September 14, 2001

Going Back Downtown

Courage is not having the strength to go on;
it is going on when you don't have the strength.
— Theodore Roosevelt

After another trip home, I drove my car back to the Academy and parked in the lot. Walking to the Bureau of Training I could feel my energy increasing in expectation of going back downtown. The flat pavement felt a little weird in relation to the pile downtown.

I thought, "Perhaps tonight would be a good night. Maybe we will find those people, wherever they are. "

I found the evening group of our team waiting in front of the building.

"What is the delay?" Rob asked.

"The Lieutenant is not sure we can have the vehicle, they may need it Saturday."

"Did you tell them it was coming back tonight?" Rob asked.

"They want to protect their vehicle. Ridiculous!" he exclaimed.

105

The Lieutenant emerged from her office and said, "I have an Academy to run. We are not here to play limousine service."

Rob said, "You're kidding right? Thousands of people are missing, including our own people, and you don't want to give us a vehicle? You know the vehicle is coming back in a couple of hours with the day crew don't you?"

Dave, an instructor from the Academy went inside to make a phone call.

Moments later Dave emerged with the keys and said, "The call came down from the Chief. Let them have the truck."

We started heading downtown. Sitting in the truck I could feel the wear on my body from walking in and around the pile. The kind of wear you feel during the first weeks of basketball practice in a new season. Boy I was sore and stiff. There was no question of backing down.

"Let's get down there and get to work," my mind commanded my body.

We arrived at Ground Zero and walked over to the medical base tent.

"Hey you pussies are back," Ralph exclaimed.

I quipped, "Us, you're the one who has to go back to your bed each night, while the real work gets done."

"Someone has to meet the President during the day," Ralph blurted out, smirking.

I took a double take and said, "What did he say?"

"No." I asked, "President Bush?"

Ralph answered, "Yup, he was here today."

I asked, "Did you get to meet him?"

Ralph said, "No, he was up on a fire truck surrounded by VIPs, but we heard him speak."

A firefighter having his hand on Ralph's shoulder looked at him and asked, "Did the Prez get dust on his shoes?"

Ralph replied, "Yes, he did. He walked down into the pit and into the mud."

The firefighter exclaimed, "Good! He will remember this and do something about this travesty."

Our team assembled by the NYPD ESU base and we waited for

the sergeant and lieutenant to come out. NYPD had some better hand lights and equipment, so we upgraded our equipment. I took a hand light and a light for my helmet. I really did not want to carry anything unnecessary. We climbed into the stake body truck and loaded our equipment. The stake body truck lurched forward with the uneven shifting.

"Goddamn Lester, get it right, it sucks back here!" a voice yelled out.

The officers chuckled and grinned.

Camaraderie is a big deal on days like this. As bad as it is losing hundreds of cops, firemen and EMS providers, we still have to work and move forward, somehow. This is uncharted water for all of us. We have all lost one or two co-workers in our career, but to lose hundreds and the World Trade Center is new ground. We will moved forward but every step was a new one and in unchartered territory.

As we walked down to the pile I saw a familiar face. Approaching us was the McDonalds manager who had given us food on the 12th for free.

He said, "Good evening sir. How are you guys doing?"

I replied to his inquiry with a slow and downbeat tone. "I don't know if I will ever be the same, ever again."

The manager asked, "Why?"

I said, "I, I don't know if I can handle going to McDonalds and paying for food again. You have spoiled us." I started smiling and we all enjoyed a good laugh.

The manager reached in his pocket and took out some coupons for a free meal at McDonalds. He said, "Take a few for each of you. You guys are amazing. I don't know how you go down there and do your jobs. Thank you. What would we do without people who know how to deal with and how to help people?"

I waved and we walked away.

I told my partner, "I do not like unearned praise. I don't know what he thinks we have been doing. There is nobody to treat or save."

Don pointed out, "We are providing a service of trying to help, doing our best. The average person does not know how to deal with these things. We provide a sense of someone doing his or her best."

"I would rather be making a difference," I replied.

He said, "We are Steve, we are doing our best and showing people we are trying everything we can to find their friends and family. We are doing our VERY best."

Don Brown Wearing USAR Personal Protective Equipment at Ground Zero

We kept walking toward the chatter of jackhammers and pay loaders that were trying to erode the pile like the ebbing tide washing over the storm wall for years. We arrived in front of Number Four World Trade Center where the construction crews were busy digging and removing steel.

We unloaded our equipment and stocked the boxes near the street.

Rescuers quickly sat on the boxes and occupied a seat for the long wait to find a void in the wreckage or victims. The rest of us waited and then leaned from one foot to the other over time.

A team member came back with a couple of dozen orange buckets for us to sit on. These five gallon buckets were a great improvised seat. It felt good to sit while we waited for victims or voids or eternity, which ever came first. My feet were pulsing from the strain and blisters; it felt good to sit down and wait. I don't know what we thought we were waiting for. Looking back at the nights of searching and waiting we were really chasing the shadow of hope.

I looked to my left and saw an officer whose name I recognized and asked, "Are you *the* David Dunn?"

He looked at me and replied, "Depends."

I said, "Hey, I have heard your name for years in EMS circles and it is nice to meet you. You're a legend in EMS."

He said, "Really, I have not been there for many years."

We chatted about EMS, the problems with the job and shared why we thought EMS was kind of caught in the rise and not as respected as NYPD or FDNY.

While we were talking I heard the call on the Radio, "May Day, May Day, May Day, fireman in a shaft Liberty and West."

Instinctively I stood up and looked towards Liberty and West. I looked as firemen were running to the distant corner of Liberty Street and West Street.

"Go ahead brother, what do you have."

The radio chirped, "We have a firefighter in a shaft about 30 feet down."

The voice reported "Ok. Help is on the way, Liberty and West firefighter down."

I looked at Dave and said, "You going to go?"

"No." he replied.

I looked at him kind of funny.

Dave continued, "Don't get me wrong, I will go to help if I am called. But, I am not going to volunteer to get abused."

I looked over at the sergeant and he looked back and said, "Looks like they have more than enough help. Besides, no freelancing."

I thought about how the FDNY team wanted to work alone and

Steve Kanarian, EMT-P, MPH FDNY EMS Lieutenant (Retired)

how we are FDNY EMS and assigned to NYPD. I thought, "What a messed up marriage this is."

Then, I sat back down and continued the wait with my team.

Destroyed Trucks and Debris
Washed and Covered

As the night wore on the darkness and damp air crept into the site. Watching the mechanical monsters move metal was very mesmerizing. A loader would pick up some metal in the edge of the pit, then and dump the, another loader would drive it to the dump area where a third loader would fill the tractor-trailer dump truck.

The construction crews had made a wooden platform and a man with rain gear and a mask was washing the trucks and debris down before it was covered. Someone had the forethought to wash and cover the trucks before they drove through Brooklyn and Manhattan to Staten Island. As the night wore on time flew and it is hard to account for the hours of waiting and watching as the cold crept in and hope faded.

Later I noticed the greyish white smoke that had been burning since the 11th was now turning acrid black. I wonder what the flames have gotten a hold of. Black smoke like that is usually from petroleum products.

I said to someone, "I hear the have all kinds of secret stuff in the Trade Center."

Another rescuer chimed in, "Yeah, right. This is just an office building, just bigger and taller."

**Mechanical Monsters Moving Metal at Ground Zero
(Photo Courtesy of Bobby Wong)**

The wind direction changed and started blowing towards us. We were sitting uphill from Ground Zero but the wind was now blowing the thick acrid black smoke into our faces. I felt my mask and made sure it fit snugly. I looked over at the team member to my right and said, "We should move."

The team member replied, "Nah, this mask will protect you form 32 different chemicals. We're fine."

I thought about the training I had in the EMS Academy and recalled the instructor's words. The average house fire has fifty different chemicals for the combustion of petroleum products, plastics and synthetics.

I thought, "This is far worse than the average house fire. There are cyanides, chemicals, carbon monoxide and God only knows what."

Time, Distance, and Shielding:
My Three Best Friends

I looked to my left and saw the sergeant. I walked over and asked him, "Mind if I go over to Burger King and wash up, use the bathroom."

He looked at me, EMS Medic right?" I nodded. Feeling the strain of my mask straps I adjusted my mask.

The sergeant answered, "Sure go ahead medic; if we need you I know where to find you."

I walked over to Burger King and entered the restaurant. There were boxes of pastry and wrapped sandwiches.

A volunteer asked me, "Are you hungry?"

I replied, "No. I would really like a cup of hot tea though."

The volunteer said, "No problem, I will make it for you."

I went into the bathroom and took my mask and coat off. I washed my face, hands, and neck and blew my nose out in the sink, right nostril, then left. I put water in the cup of my palm and sucked it up into my nose. Repeating the process until the water was clear. I rinsed my face with hot water and felt better. I washed the rubber lining of my mask with hot water. I put some soap in my mask to have something better to smell.

I went back into the restaurant and got my tea. Sipping my tea I sat on the stool. I could see the Burger King decorations and colors that had been covered with makeshift signs and black and white maps of Ground Zero. I finished my tea and walked outside.

The smoke was still blowing in our direction. I turned right and stood by the building facing away from Ground Zero. The brick wall had retained heat from the warm sunny day, and I felt secure leaning against an intact building that was warm.

During our terrorism response training we were taught principles of safety. We had learned the common characteristics of a terrorist incident and the three rules of safety. We learned to use Time, Distance, and Shielding. The concept was to limit your time exposed to a hazard, maximize your distance, and use the best shielding. I was fortunate to have a filter mask, turnout gear, and good training. Right now I was using the best shielding, a large, intact brick building.

I felt secure for the first time in several days. I looked over toward the team and the sergeant gave me the thumbs up as if to say, "I see you, I know where you are." I thought, for now I am going to stay with my three best friends, Time, Distance, and Shielding.

Sun Rising Over the Horizon.
Waiting for Relief

The sun began to creep up over the horizon and the long fingers of lights again slowly embraced the buildings, as a hand would comfort an injury. Morning was here. A newspaper truck came by, stopped, and dropped off a bundle of papers at the command post. Firemen and police officers began to walk over to get coffee and look at the morning paper. This was one of the only familiar routines from everyday life here at Ground Zero; the rest of our world had been turned over.

"When is our country going to bomb the shit out of these terrorists? What are they waiting for?" a fireman asked as he was folding the paper in half and placing it under his arm as he walked, stirring his hot coffee. I could see wisps of warmth evaporate into the desolate air and disappear as he walked back to the pile.

We had to wait for our relief to come to the tent. I decided to take a walk and look around during the daylight. I walked out onto Broadway and saw volunteers who had set up in the street. There were cases of water on tables with food and supplies.

I just walked around and took my mask off. I pushed my hair back off my forehead and felt the warm sun on my face. I saw people coming in and out of St. Paul's Chapel. I walked into the chapel and looked around. There were some rescuers resting and some people praying. "Dear God why have you done this to us? Give me the strength to persevere." I imagined I could see the thoughts in their minds.

I sat and thought about what we were experiencing. I saw a sign that said, "This is where George Washington sat during the revolutionary war." The white colonial woodwork was soothing and reflected the light from the outside. Somehow I felt a lighter burden. I snapped up and returned to the base camp.

Kevin Enright and His Partner

I walked out into the street and watched all of the commotion as the morning pace was picking up. I looked around and saw volunteers reporting for work, and rescuers who had been on the pile walking back for relief. In front of me I saw two EMS EMTs walking by. I waived to Kevin Enright and his partner. No response at all.

"That little prick," I thought. "I will never give him another mutual schedule change again." Then I realized that I was dressed differently and he probably did not recognize me in USAR garb.

I walked behind him without notice, and I put my hand on his shoulder from behind and said, "Good Morning Kevin."

Kevin jumped and reeled around. "What the ..."

I took off my mask and smiled.

Kevin exclaimed, "Bossman, you are in the shit aren't you?"

I replied, "Yes I am Kevin, there is a lot of shit here to wade through brother."

He said, "So glad to see you, we were wondering how you were doing down here."

I replied, "There is a lot of work to be done Kevin. Not many patients but a lot of work."

He shook my hand and added, "Nice to see you Bossman. Hurry back we miss you at the station."

I said, "Thank you Kevin, I will."

Looking back at the events of the days after September 11, 2001 now, it may seem like we did not do much. I don't know where the time went during the many hours of walking and searching and standing and waiting. The event was in a lot of ways a blur of activity. Chief Martin told me that he could not recall many hours of intense work and continuous decision-making.

Either it is a defense mechanism or our minds way of protecting us from the excruciating details and horror. The time did become a blur, but the things we remember seeing are unforgettable.

IX

Night of Searching.
Saturday September 15, 2001

W e returned to the World Trade Center site again, for another night of physically exhausting work. I was tired and weary. Jack and Lou were talking outside the tent. They were drinking Coke and eating McDonalds. "Wow, signs of normal life," I thought.

"Where did you get that?" I asked.

"Around the corner. But they are all out of Coke," Jack stated.

My mood dropped. I thought, "I have been drinking water for a few days. It would have been nice. To have a Coke." I walked around the corner and saw the McDonalds trailer. There was a short line and rescuers were walking up and taking a couple of sandwiches and fries, which were all free.

"Nice," I thought.

I saw the bucket where the drinks were. I reached into the searing cold, icy water and hoped there was water left. *I felt cans*! I pulled out a Coke, then another Coke. Jack Quigley had been joking about the Coke not being left.

I thought, *"Damn!"*

I returned to the tent with two Cokes and two burgers.

Captain Jack was laughing and the others were smirking. Jack and Lou played a simple practical joke, playing with my emotions to break the monotony.

"*It is all good,*" I thought.

I guess the Coke made me feel alive and reminded me of the beach and good times, happy times. Not to mention the sugar would provide some good short-term energy to get me moving.

Central Park Unit Volunteers Including Tina Dunn, an Unidentified EMT, and Andrew Skomorfsky Working at the WTC Site on 9/15 (Photo courtesy of Bobby Wong)

Back on the Pile

"Maybe tonight I would get to man the medical tent," I thought.

My feet hurt, my back was sore, my legs were sore from trying to walk over the severe angles of metal. I could feel the weight of the pack on my shoulders despite the pack not being there.

When I arrived at the base camp I saw some team members already checking their equipment and vying for positions.

One said, "I will do supply, I got medical tent."

"Listen to these guys," I thought.

Sure enough Captain Booth's roll call confirmed what I had thought, back on the pile again.

"Damn," I thought as I got up and briskly walked over to Captain Booth and said, "You know Jim, I would love to stay in the tent one night too. I feel like a shmuck going out every night."

Jim looked around and behind him and said, "Steve I want you with me out there, on the pile. We are going to look for my cousin's husband who was a cop. They think they know where he is. I want you with me. I know how you work. You were my partner."

I thought, "Cool, I am wanted, someone wants my help."

Suddenly I felt revived and a little energetic. My pain faded away and I leaned into the assignment.

"Hell!" I thought, "This is not going to last forever. I want to go out *every* night, *every* minute and make the difference, get the job done! There will be time to rest later."

We continued getting our equipment ready, signing out radios and checking flashlights. In this environment you need a light and a back up light, and water and a good pair of gloves. I changed the cartridge on my mask from yesterday. I wiped toothpaste along the mask for a change from the rubber smell.

A fire Captain came into the tent with his hand wrapped in a bloody t-shirt.

"Can I help you Cap?" I asked.

"Yes, I cut my hand." he replied.

"When did this happen?" I asked.

"Yesterday." The Captain said. Then he stared at the ground and was speechless.

I unwrapped his hand and began to wash the wound. Watching his affect the whole time I noticed he did not move his eyes away from the ground.

"You OK Boss?" I inquired.

He turned his head up and to the side a little, never leaving the hunched over position and said, "They say there are two airplanes here. I have not seen either one."

I replied, "I know, the only airplane part I saw was a landing wheel in a dumpster marked 'Airplane parts,' It's messed up Captain." I rinsed his hand and wrapped the wound.

Dr. Gonzales looked at the wound and exclaimed, "What are you doing? You can't go back to work, you have to get that hand sutured and get antibiotics. You know what junk is that pile?"

The Captain answered, "That is OK. I will deal with it."

Dr. Gonzales said, "You could lose your hand if you don't get that taken care of. Think about it. You're a fireman; you crawl around in this crap when these buildings are on fire. When they collapse all the sewerage and air duct mold is out in the open. There are feces, blood, chemicals and germs from the air vents all over, not to mention whatever else we don't know about. I promise you this, if you do not go, I will have you medically restricted and you will not be able to come back down here at all."

The captain responded, "That is OK, I will deal with it later."

Dr. Gonzales stated, "You are going to the hospital or I will restrict you medical."

The Captain replied, "Ok, I will go to the hospital. Can I come back to dig when I am done?"

The doctor replied, "Yes, just take the antibiotics and keep the hand wrapped."

The Captain said, "Thanks Doc. You're right. My head is somewhere else."

The doctor told him, "I know brother; we all feel the same way."

Staging at Number 5 World Trade Center

Jim called out to me, saying "Steve. Let's go." We walked over to the PD command post and met our team for the night. Jim talked to the sergeant and I started to climb in back of the stake body truck.

I heard, "Where you going?" I looked to my side and saw that a PD lieutenant from ESU was asking me that question.

"I am with the team," I replied.

The lieutenant replied, "I know, you ride up front. You're a medic and a lieutenant, get up front."

I said, "I don't mind."

The lieutenant said "Really get in the cab. You deserve to ride up front."

"Thanks Lieutenant." I replied.

It felt good to sit and be out of the moist fall air. The seat felt good. Although it was a vinyl seat with the springs pushing through, it was something other than ground or steel. The truck drove up West Street and turned on Chambers.

I thought, *"Wow. We're moving.* The streets are clearer and we can actually move around."

Then, we stopped, unloaded the truck and prepared for another night's work.

Volunteer EMT Assisting with Mask at WTC Site
(Photo Courtesy of Bobby Wong)

As we walked I started singing to myself, "Downtown, where the lights are out all night. Downtown, where there is not a soul." "Downtown" I sang out loud, "where the lights are out all night."

We smiled and realized the everyday life we knew was forever changed. The twin towers were gone. The fire chiefs, Chief Downey and the rescue guys that led the way were gone. Our world was forever changed.

The Massachusetts State Trooper

We were staging outside of Number Five World Trade Center to go into the subway to look to search the area for victims. We were waiting for a generator so we could run lights in the subway. As we waited the rain started to fall lightly. Rain drops slashed in the dust but made no impact. The clean water and poisonous dust separated.

I looked around and saw a familiar but out of place sight. "Could it really be?" I thought. I looked to my left and saw a Massachusetts State trooper. I looked at his characteristic light blue Triangular patch with the Massachusetts State seal on it. I could not believe I was standing there with a trooper from my home state, there on Broadway and Church Street in Manhattan.

Growing up in suburban Massachusetts the police had very little contact with the public. The state police had even less contact unless you got pulled over for speeding. The Massachusetts trooper uniform is very intimidating. They wear a coat, which is tailored to a "V" shape in the back, and boots that have a raised profile to gain the height advantage.

I looked over and nodded to the trooper who was shorter and younger than me. This trooper also had a German shepherd with him on a leash.

I said, "Good evening sir, how are you."

He replied, "Ok."

"What are you doing here?" I inquired.

He replied curtly and quickly, "I am here to search for bodies."

I again asked, "I know, but what are you doing *here* from *Massachusetts*?" I adjusted my stance and turned towards him and added, "I can understand Enfield Connecticut, Fort Lee police, but you're from three states away. What are you doing here from Massachusetts?"

The trooper clenched his jaw and I noticed how the muscles in his jaw hardened and he swallowed distastefully. I could sense his anger and seriousness. "Sir, those planes came from our airport, we are responsible for this," he said as he looked around encompassing the destruction in front of us.

I thought, "That is an awesome burden he was feeling. That will be a feeling he will live with the rest of his life I am sure." It is not easy dealing with the "What if" questions in quiet places after the job is over. I sensed a change in conversation would be welcome.

"What do you think of New York City?" I asked the trooper.

He replied, "I am used to Boston, sir. Manhattan blows away Boston. I cannot even comprehend this disaster."

"Want me to blow your mind again?" I asked the trooper.

"That is not possible sir," he said.

"I am from Rehoboth Massachusetts," I said as I looked at him to watch his reaction. He looked at me quizzically.

I told him, "I started volunteering in Rehoboth and went to the Northeastern University paramedic program. I came here for field rotations and never left."

"Well, you did it," he remarked. "I am from Assonet."

Assonet was a few towns over and we used to play against them in basketball. I thought, "Wow, whoever would have thought that I would be on an assignment in Manhattan with a Massachusetts state trooper?" I reached down and let his German shepherd smell my hand and then I petted the dog. The irony struck me that here I was in Manhattan talking to a Massachusetts State trooper who was younger and smaller than me. I was struck by his show of emotion and anger. I had never seen emotion form a trooper growing up. My how times have changed from when I was younger.

The California USAR Team

As we waited I noticed a group of firefighters coming around the corner from the area between the two buildings. These firefighters were wearing yellow turn out pants and bunker pants. I realized these were not New York City firemen. As they came closer I noticed that this team had the cuffs of their pants and coats taped with duct tape to keep dust and debris out. I could tell by the way they held their tools and the way their equipment was well worn that this team had experience.

I thought, "This team knows their shit!"

As they got closer I saw the markings of a California USAR team.

"Wow!" I thought, "these are the guys who responded to the Loma Prieta Earthquake."

California had several USAR teams because of the potential loss from earthquakes. As they drew nearer our ESU lieutenant approached the captain of the team and asked, "What are you guys doing here?"

The captain replied, "If we do not belong here let us know. FDNY did not want us in the pit."

"Wow!" I thought, "This is the second largest department in the country, why wouldn't they want their help in the pit?"

The ESU lieutenant removed his helmet and scratched his forehead and said, "I would be glad to have your help here." They shook hands then the team members exchanged greetings and mutual complements.

One of them said, "Sorry for your losses Lieutenant."

I replied, "Thank you, thanks for coming."

The ESU lieutenant began to explain, pointing to the basement of the building, "Under this building is the subway. Because of the collapse we cannot gain entry. We are going to try again tonight to enter the subway. It needs to be searched and we can get out of the rain for the night."

"Sounds like a plan," the fire captain from California said.

Soon thereafter a truck returned with several generators and some fuel.

"Move out men. We are going down into the subway," the Lieutenant stated.

A sense of mission filled the air and we began to move into Number 5 World Trade Center. Walking down the marble hallway we could feel how vacant the building as. On any given day or evening these buildings would be teaming with thousands of people who were going to work, important meetings or to a lunch meeting. The silence was very obvious.

A "crack" noise radiated through the atrium as a team member broke a stone tile that had fallen. We walked down the escalator with team members on both sides walking down into the darkness. One by one lights came on and filled the subway corridor.

"We will stage here, give me "A" team. We will make entry into the subway through that debris and we will see what we can get access to."

The "A" team worked hard digging and filling buckets that were sent back to the hallway and dumped out. They dug with anticipation and hope of breaking into the subway. There had been rumors that an officer was trapped with five civilians in the subway. A 911 caller stated they needed help.

I thought, "Maybe tonight would be the night."

As the digging continued the building creaked slightly as the wind and rain intensified outside. The rain was blistering the earth and buildings and, hopefully, washing away the dust and putting those damn fires out.

The digging continued. The team stood by quietly. There was no more idle chit chat. There were no more golly gee remarks or topics to pretend to be interested in. We were tired and focused. We were determined not to stop until we found everybody. Yet, there were no positive signs of life. We were not even finding many bodies.

The rain intensified and the building began to creak regularly then groan a little. The building appeared to be safe but one had to take note of the wind and noises coming from the building. I knew there would come a point where this rescue operation got dangerous, real dangerous. Now we were at that point.

"Shit!" an officer called out as a cloud of dust filled the hole they were digging in the ground. "Ok, Yeah, Jesus, right down my back."

"Ok, back to work, dig!" exclaimed the ESU sergeant who was built like a Tiger Tank. He was here to make a difference and you could see he was not going to stop. Buckets where coming out of the hole regularly and more and more men where slipping into the hole to extend the bucket brigade.

The building groaned some more and I was now watching the atrium ceiling that was some seventy feet above us. Looking for movement, fissures, whatever would give me warning. The firemen who taught our building collapse class at Randall's Island said, "Before a building collapses, it talks to you. It tells you to get the hell out. Doors and windows begin to rack and break, doors sometimes open on their own accord." I was watching the doors and they were not moving.

A voice chirped over the PD radio, "62.4."

"What?" another voice asked.

The voice on the radio answered, "I said, 62.4."

"What the hell is that?" the other voice asked.

The response was, "The weight of a cubic foot of water is 62.4 pounds."

Simultaneously, we all started calculating the weight bearing down on this structure. I am guessing the building is maybe 400 feet by 250 feet, the parapet is probably two to three feet high. "Shit!" I thought. The exact math was not important, nor possible to calculate in this late hour in this state of exhaustion. That is a lot of water.

The tension grew and we were wondering what was next.

"Is this where the story ends?" I was thinking.

A "Cr-rack" noise filled the atrium and I looked upward in time to see a 40-foot gash in the dry wall split open and hundreds of pounds of dry wall and rock came down onto the floor. We were all up against the wall and a good distance from the collapse. I bumped into another guy and apologized. Looking over at him, I saw he was against another guy who was up against the wall by the door. Subconsciously we had all been shuffling out near the entrance of the atrium by the escalators.

"ESU base to all ESU teams." The radio crackled with some squelch and distortion. "We are suspending operations for the night. All ESU teams are to acknowledge the order to cease operations and give their name of the Lieutenant in charge."

The radio came alive.

"Team 1 acknowledge, Lieutenant McNally."

"Team 2 acknowledge, Lieutenant Smith."

"Team 4 acknowledge, Lieutenant Callahan."

A long palpable pause filled the air. "ESU base to Team 3, acknowledge message to cease operations."

The silence continued. We could see the sergeant and he was holding his radio saying, "Di-ig, I said, Dig."

The team continued to dig.

An alert tone pierced the air and the radio quipped, "ESU base to Team 3, acknowledge the order to cease operations, give the lieutenant's name."

Someone's head pointed out from the hole and he said, "It is no use, Sir. We are up against concrete floors that slid down from above; there are two or three in a row. It is impossible without serious equipment."

The sergeant took off his helmet and wiped his forehead, a greyish streak formed in the sweat. "Ok, Ok. Get out of there. Let's go home. ESU Base Team 3 acknowledges your order, Lieutenant O'Brien is team leader."

"10–4 Team 3."

We drove back to the ESU base and walked inside as someone said, "Come on in EMS. Relax, we will go back out later when the rain dies down." I was relieved to take off my pack and stretch my back. Without that equipment I felt light enough to float.

I saw John McCullough. "Hey John, how are you?"

He replied, "I don't know Steve. This sucks. We can't find these guys and now the weather won't let us work."

I said, "I thought that was the point of no return in there tonight."

He smiled, "Nahh, that is just Pat being Pat. The guys love him to death because he never backs down. During our training we are always taught not to trade cops for bodies. Now if there is a kid or a cop who needs help, all bets are off, but what's the use of losing more cops in a mess like this. None. Get some rest Steve."

"John, it bothers me that people are thanking us for what we are doing. On the inside of this mess there's nobody to recue. Nothing good is happening."

John replied, "I know how you feel. I think that they are saying thank you for doing something that they can't do themselves. They are thanking us because they are helpless and cannot begin to think about how they would handle this type of disaster. We do the job they can't do. I think there is always hope that someone will be found alive; hope that a loved one will be saved. Or at least a loved one will be found."

I sat down and rested, but was aware of all the noises in the auditorium and how many people were there.

A strong hand shook my shoulder, and I heard, "EMS go on back to your base. We are done for the night."

"What time is it?" I asked. I heard, "03:45 and the weather prediction is for continued rain and high winds."

"Oh, ok," I replied. "Good Night."

The 1993 World Trade Center Bombing

As I was resting, I started thinking about the 1993 bombing of the World Trade Center. When it happened, I was at Floyd Bennet Field taking load planning training for the USAR team. Just before lunch the firemen started making their way to the kitchen. I thought it was to get a jump on lunch. We finally broke for lunch and headed for the kitchen. The firemen were huddled around the TV watching the newsreel footage of the Trade Center burning and talking among themselves.

"Must be a generator, look at the color of that smoke."

"Those brothers are eating smoke down there."

"Yup. *What the hell are we doing here? We should be down there.*"

As the afternoon passed we learned that the World Trade Center had been bombed, there were a few fatalities and hundreds of patients. A firefighter had fallen four stories into the pit and was being rescued. We were directed to respond to the Trade Center after class to help out.

At this particular time the USAR team was a team that had to assemble equipment from stations across the city. In essence, the USAR team had to scrounge to get equipment. FEMA only pays after a deployment. We responded to the Trade Center and joined the special operations people already at work. We essentially stood by in case there were trapped victims found in the rubble.

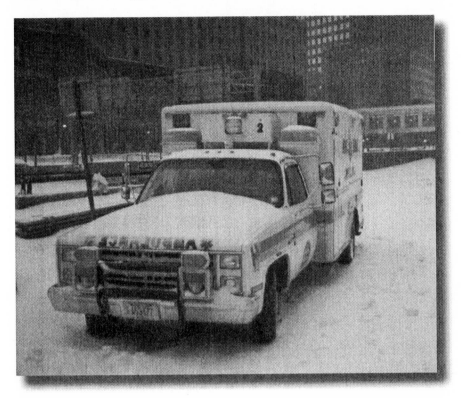

USAR Ambulance at Twin Towers after 1993 Bombing

For me being in Manhattan and not being assigned to 911 calls was a break from the rigors of Bronx EMS and having very little time to relax. Day after day we stood by and watched as the investigation progressed and the pit was uncovered. I was amazed to see how thorough and complete the blast damage was. We noticed road signs that were at a right angle to the parking garage entrance. These signs were blown away from the wall by the blast.

ESU Truck 3 in Front of Twin Towers after 1993 Bombing

We were standing by one day when Chief Maniscalco came out of the trailer and said, "Get some equipment, get your coat on, we are going inside."

I wondered what was up.

Chief Maniscalco was focused and in a hurry.

"What's up chief?" I asked. "They found a body, need a pronouncement."

We went into the pit and down the path of debris to where the seventh victim was found. The patient was obviously dead and had been entombed in debris. Looking at the scene I was impressed at how the brick walls had been broken down completely to the individual brick. I would imagine an explosion would leave parts of a brick wall intact, but what I was seeing was complete and through devastation.

We confirmed the person was dead and exchanged the cursory information.

"Thanks." the officer replied.

On the way out Chief Maniscalco asked me, "Have you seen the truck?"

"What truck?" I asked.

He replied, "The rental truck?"

"No, it is intact?" I asked.

He told me walk quickly and do not look around. We walked briskly into a secure area in the Trade Center garage. There in the garage FBI technicians had taken apart a Ryder van to compare parts with the parts being found on the scene.

"How cool!" I thought. "The FBI has a reputation for painstaking detail when collecting evidence. This was the FBI in action. Very cool."

As I mentally compared the two incidents, I realized that the 1993 terrorist incident was overshadowed by the horrific events of September 11th. Now I could see what total devastation of the Trade Center was really like.

Bill McCabe

In 1993 my good friend Bill McCabe was working in the World Trade Center for Saint Vincent's Hospital ambulance as a paramedic with his partner Garrett Doering. Bill and Garret were stationed at the Port Authority Police Sub–station in the sub basement when the bomb went off. Bill and Garrett were confronted with thick acrid smoke in the basement, but they still were able to start treating Port Authority employees who were injured. They considered going into the devastation to look for missing employees but realized they were in a very unsafe environment. Instead, Bill and Garrett drove the Port Authority employees out of the sub-basement in the ambulance. When they reached daylight, they stopped and told EMS units arriving who they were and where they had been. Then they transported their patients to the hospital.

In retrospect I am amazed at the different aspects of the World Trade Center story I have been involved in and the people I know who have these amazing stories to share. I am grateful my friend Bill is OK. I feel blessed to have never lost any of my close friends at work.

X
Another Night at Ground Zero.
Sunday September 16, 2001

Ground Zero Quiet

We came in to work and found certain solitude at the Ground Zero site. Sundays are usually busy days for EMS in the Bronx. This area of Manhattan was unusually quiet. My guess was that the public realized there were no more people to rescue. The job was now recovering bodies and finding clues. There was a faint hope that a patient or two may be found alive, but the longest survivor from a collapse to date had been 48 hours. We were well past the 48 hour window now.

For the first time public attention seemed to be returning to everyday life for the public. Maybe people were realizing that it was Sunday and they needed rest and had to laundry. Perhaps people were getting ready for the upcoming week. Nonetheless, Ground Zero was quiet. For those missing family members, co-workers brothers and sisters Ground Zero was the only thing concerning them.

While were standing by the rescue work on West Street I saw a tall ESU cop whom I had known for years. I went out of my way say hello and shake hands. I have never known Too Tall's name or conversed much with him. The extent of our professional relationship was a nod of mutual respect on heavy jobs and shared competency.

"Good to see you sir," I said.

He replied, "Likewise. How have you been?"

"Good." I answered.

I exclaimed, "Jeez! We have been doing job together for like 20 years."

"Yup," he responded.

I asked To Tall, "What was the worst job you ever did?"

He replied with the qualifying question, " Do you mean shooting, pin job or Rescue?"

A pin job is a term used to describe a call where a patient is crushed in a car and unable to get out. Rescue crews will use pneumatic or hydraulic rescue tools to peel back the car door and dashboard to gain entry to the patient. In severe cases where the patient needs to be immediately extricated from the wreck, rescuers will cut the six supports of the roof and remover the whole roof.

I replied, "I guess pin jobs."

I realized most of the good shootings are in the news anyway; let me see what accidents he is impressed with.

To Tall said, "The worst pin job I have been on was the EMS accident of Pelham Parkway."

I nodded and said, "I know that accident."

A good friend of mine, Tim, was on that accident where the ambulance left the roadway late at night and struck a tree in the median. The driver was pinned so severely they could only reach him through the rear compartment of the ambulance. Tim had told me, "I could only reach in and put a non-rebreather on him."

I agreed that was a bad one.

Too Tall continued, "I did not think they would make it. It was a real bad wreck. The way the ambulances were wrapped over him I thought he was dead. An ambulance is made of hard metal, not like your average car. To have that amount of damage was impressive."

I nodded in agreement. I had seen the pictures of that ambulance. I listened as Too Tall described some of the elaborate searches, hostage negotiating jobs and rescues he had been on. I had known Too Tall for many years and there was a sense of mutual respect in each other's roles. We had never spoken much except, "EMS, what do you need? Can you cut the roof, this guy is bad? You got it EMS." The hydraulic generator would ramp up in speed and you could hear the machine strain as the metal resisted them buckle under pressure. I'd hear, "Thanks."

Who would have ever thought that we would all be down here together in the World Trade Center looking for hundreds of coworkers and civilians? In all of our conversation the Trade Center did not come up as the worst of any job. This response was clearly different, incomparable to any experience any of us have had.

Too Tall walked away and I looked over the scene at Ground Zero. The sun was low in the sky and the last rays of warmth were receding. There were sounds of machinery but they were on a less grand scale. People where realizing here were no more victims to rescue, the job was now recovering bodies and finding clues. Sunday evenings in EMS are usually busy in the Bronx.

"The Spirit of New York"

During our nightly briefing Captain Booth told us we would be working independently in zones tonight rather than going with teams to perform entries. He said, "The emphasis is now shifting to the pile on West Street. All buildings that can be searched have been searched."

There was a buzz about "The Spirit of New York" being opened tonight for rescuers and volunteers. Unfortunately, the ship was located on the other side of the pile behind the World Financial Center and it would be a long walk over the debris pile to get to the ship.

Lou and I walked from the tent and headed around the pile, we walked by Ten House where there were wreaths and monuments in front. There were notes of sympathy and patches from around the country on the wall. The Ten House was a focal point of sympathy for firemen who were lost. FDNY Ten house was across the street from the pile. Can't get any closer than that.

We walked over debris stopping periodically to check in with EMS officers and medics we knew along the way. It was refreshing to see people we used to work with who had transferred to different parts of the city, people you had not seen in years. Even though we do not really acknowledge it every day, we are all one big team who look out for each other. They will seldom admit it, but down deep we all care about one another. The daily quibbles and arguments sometimes get in the way.

Hell! Being tired and working under emergency conditions will put the best of friends in an argument. But in the wake of an event like September 11th all of those trivial things faded away. Policemen and firefighters were even working hand in hand now. They have had their share of arguments in the past, but under the circumstances we were all pulling in one direction.

Lou and I walked behind the World Financial Center and around the back. The air was clear and the grass was green, there was no dust or debris. The grass was soft and the earth was a welcome relief to walking on concrete and metal. The air was dust free. Being behind the World Financial Center was like being in an oasis from Hell.

We walked toward the ship and I felt a little reluctant to go in. The ship was magnificent large cruise ship that was used for weddings and executive parties off the coast of New York. This ship was exclusive. I felt funny walking in with my boots and equipment that was worn and dust covered. As I approached the gangplank a waitress approached us and said, "Welcome. Come on in and relax. We appreciate all you have been doing."

I replied, "Thank you. I would hate to ruin your rug."

She said, "That is ok. We can clean it. Make yourself at home."

I put my backpack and turnout coat on the floor against the wall. There were small groups of rescuers spread around the floor of the ship. I walked over to the buffet and saw an assortment of food, roast beef, vegetables, rice and deserts. I asked for some chicken marsala and rice, and then sat at our table. I ate some food and looked around. The bright lights and colored table clothes were a welcome site. The fabric on the table was coarse but a welcome sensation. I wiped my lips with a linen napkin and put my fork down. I enjoyed a few bites of food and the taste but really was not hungry.

Destroyed Rescue Vehicles Being
Washed and Crushed

Lou and I walked back to the site of activity on West Street and took up a position to stand by. There was intense activity of West Street being done by hand tools and manpower. The large machines were working on the other side of the pile where the tons of I-beams had piled up to form a large sea of metal. The burned and rusted metal I-beams looked like the gate to Hell itself. I started referring to the scene as the devils mouth. Closer to us workers were uncovering debris and pulling out vehicles from a collapsed area in the street.

I saw a crane pulling a fire truck out of the pit and placing it on the ground. The fire truck was destroyed beyond use for any possible function. An excavator then pulled the vehicle away. Next, a large Fire Rescue truck was pulled out of the pit and dropped on the ground. To my surprise the vehicle was washed with hoses and it returned to its proud boastful red, yellow and white color scheme. Without hesitation the excavator crushed the severely damaged rescue truck and prepared the vehicle to be loaded and removed.

I was shocked to see a rescue company vehicle like that destroyed and written off. As I watched the scene unfold I thought of the firefighters I have seen donning equipment in the rear of the truck as they make their way to a scene of a working fire or rescue job. I wondered which rescue firefighters have been killed.

I remembered conversations I had during USAR training. "Hey, your turnout gear is new."

"Yours looks like you have been in the shit, lets go in the shit together."

"How many of those men where lost?" I wondered.

Each time a fire truck was removed from the pit and cleaned and crushed, I cringed. These were the chariots that carried heroes to save peoples lives. These were the trucks they depended on. Now they were all lost. Consumed by terrorism.

The idea that the World Trade Center was gone, these firemen where gone and the trucks destroyed was like a tale of falling heroes in mythology. The excavator continued to crunch fire trucks and then load them onto tractor-trailers.

Removing the fire trucks and washing them off, somehow, was worse because you could see their unit numbers and the unit logos displayed with pride and boasting. However, their truck was destroyed. These trucks were huge ladder towers and rescue companies. I had always thought these trucks were the biggest and "baddest" trucks in the city. Now here they were being removed from the scene like flattened tin cans. This was truly a shame, and something unbelievable was unfolding before our eyes.

We had spent many hours waiting, watching and hoping for patients to be uncovered. Gradually over the weekend the hope disappeared and frustration crept into all of us. The realization was becoming obvious that nobody had survived the collapse. There was an occasional account of an officer that rode the wreckage down from above and survived, or a woman who was pulled from the wreckage. But there were few stories of people surviving. There were no voids that had people or rescuers in them, waiting to be rescued. As we waited and hope faded, frustration set in.

XI

Turning the Bend.
Monday September 17, 2001

W e were standing in front of number 5 World Trade Center again. I really do not even remember how we got there. It is all a blur. I leaned against a large pile of timbers that had been brought in to shore up the streets and subways. I looked at Captain Quigley to my left and asked, "Jack what are we doing here?"

He said, "I don't know Steve. Gotta love the aroma though. We are not going to find anyone else in here, it has been too long and these bodies in the pile are decomposing."

I continued to sit on pile with Jack Quigley.

There was a feeling of general uneasiness, an antsy feeling. People were snapping at each other.

Captain Booth came around the corner and asked, "Jim what are we doing?"

"PD is looking for egress to the subway system from this building," Jim replied.

"No, Jim," the Captain answered.

I asked, "What are we still doing here? There is nobody left alive. EMS's job is done."

The Captain replied, "Don't forget Steve, we are also here for the rescuers. Having a New York City paramedic here is welcome for ESU officers and firefighters going in and out of these wrecked buildings."

I stood up straighter and said, "Yeah, your right. We're here for them too." I felt my mission was now somewhat clearer.

Commotion among Rescuers

We lined up and assembled by the entryway to the building and stood by again. A commotion erupted in the side alcove of the building, which resulted in some pushing and separation of the crowd of rescuers.

One person said, "What did you say?"

Another answered, "You heard me. You are thieves!"

Emotions boiled over and yelling erupted from both sides.

I moved closer to see what the commotion was.

"What's up?" I asked.

A team member replied, "One of the soldiers accused us of stealing watches from the jewelry store. Us, NYPD! You believe that shit!"

I saw the emotion boiling over and the decision of what side I would stand on caught me off guard. The US military or the NYPD? I am on both sides I thought. I am an American. In an instant I realized I have worked with ESU for years and we depend on each other. I will get behind the biggest ESU cop I can find and hit whoever comes my way. Plus, I know I will see the ESU cops again.

Someone yelled, "Wait, wait!" The crowd was pushing and facing off for a brawl disregarding the plea to stop.

"Lieutenant, I am on the job! I work in Brooklyn." The group paused and looked at the National Guardsman as he repeated, "Lieutenant, I am a sergeant in Brooklyn. I am on the job!"

The crowd of ESU officers stopped for the sergeant who was in National Guard uniform.

Someone said, "Lou, look that guy is an asshole. We all do not feel that way. We are the same Lou. He has issues."

The Lieutenant moved back his helmet and wiped his forehead. While he thought, we all waited and watched.

Just as rapidly as the group had polarized and confronted each other, the two groups dissolved and resumed their duties at hand. We descended down the steps and the soldiers returned to guarding the street and entrance.

I exhaled long and hard. I thought, "Who would have ever thought I would have to choose between the US military and NYPD ESU. This disaster has pushed us all further in every direction than any of us could have thought reasonable. Of course, this is not a reasonable incident. This is one of the worst days in American History."

The Sub-Basement Levels

We searched the sub-basement levels of the building and found markings from USAR teams from different parts of the country. "*Salt Lake City 0 bodies, 0 victims. Hazards, water, power and rodents.*"

"Welcome home," I thought. "Who is coordinating this recovery? Obviously each agency is doing its own thing. We had covered the same area and we all found nothing. Where have these people gone?"

As we walked through the building we found a breach in the wall and walked through. As we walked I realized we were in a store. Everything was covered in dust. I had the feeling I had been here before. I had never shopped down here before. I had only been to the Trade Center once or twice, on the observation tower.

I looked back and saw the breach in the concrete to the outside I thought, "That is the spot where I was on the 12th, looking in at the crypt and death. The fine delineation between death and life was interrupted. Now it is just cold death everywhere. The store no longer looked operational. The clothes were all covered with dust and debris. The last wisps of life have left this place, bringing with them the bodies and souls of the victims."

The realization was becoming clear. There were no more patients. There were no victims to find. Hope had evaporated leaving behind it in its wake the reality of the devastation was blooming. There is a huge loss of life and only the removal of debris and waste is left. Hopefully, we can find pieces of people and coworkers to say, *yes we have found them.*

We completed our foray into desperation and came out of the

ground in the middle of the construction zone. Jackhammers where stating to chatter, Brrrruup, Brrrup. Excavators where in position relaying debris from the center to the edge and then loaded onto trucks. Firefighters stood by looking for body parts and removing debris. We took up a position to wait and watch wondering what we had done to deserve this.

"We were supposed to be the wining team," I thought.

The Unconscious Rescue Dog

Rob and I heard someone shouting, "Medic, Medic." We looked over across the pile and saw a group waving for help. We started walking toward their position. When we arrived Rob asked, "What is wrong?"

A construction worker answered, "There is a dog unconscious. I think he is having a seizure."

Rob pushed his way into the crowd and looked at the dog and said, "He is definitely having a seizure, eyes are deviated to the right and front legs and neck are stiff. What happened?"

"We were searching below for bodies and Rex started acing funny. He was uncoordinated and sluggish. My guess is he inhaled some toxic fumes."

Rob said, "Steve, set me up with an IV and D50."

I ran through and intravenous set and prepared some 50% Dextrose for Rob to give the dog.

"A man pushed through the circle of people and said, "I am a vet. What is going on?"

Rob replied, "We have a 4 year old German Shepherd named Rex who is having a seizure. We believe he inhaled some toxic fumes below grade. We are setting up an IV and getting ready to give him some Dextrose."

The Vet said, "Great. Complete that treatment and we will get him out of here to the Vet Station we have set up in our trailer."

Rob applied the venous constricting band and searched for an IV site. He put the catheter into the vein and got a return of blood. We connected the IV and then pushed the Dextrose. We loaded the dog, oxygen and equipment into a stokes basket and handed the dog to the

Vet. The line of people passed the stokes basket and Rex down line to the outside, and then he disappeared into the perimeter."

I exclaimed, "You're awesome Rob. It is like you did that a hundred times."

He replied, "It is just like a hairy patient Steve."

We finally got to take care of a patient. A dog albeit.

Well, it was a rescue dog. They are like partners to the handlers.

The blue sky and nice September weather was a sarcastic background for the devastation and heartbreak. It would be more appropriate if there were heavy rains and thunder like in the movies. This is not a movie though, this is reality and life is not always clear. Ambiguity was what hangs us up mentally and makes us wonder in our quiet moments. I had the feeling we will be dwelling on this job for a long time.

Leaving Ground Zero

Later in the night we met for the roll call at the medical team base as the day team arrived. Dr. Gonzales announced, "I am getting a lot of flak for having so many of you guys here. We need for some of you to return to the Borough." I looked around and nobody was budging.

I said, "Doctor, I will go back. I am a lieutenant; my station needs me. Let some of the medics stay and do their job."

He replied, "Thanks Kanarian, report to your station tomorrow, Tour 2. Jimmy will let them know your coming back."

I thought, "What? Not even a few days off? Just like Hurricane George — full out for 24 hours a day and then back to the station the next morning. Duty calls."

The briefing continued about what type of cranes were being brought in and discussions held between FEMA and the Office of Emergency Management. Passes with photos were being handed out and I felt that Ground Zero was taking on a whole new direction, a life of its own. I could feel the split in the tracks, so to speak, and I wanted no part in being here anymore. I wanted to go back to my station were I could actually make a difference.

Knowing this was my last trip out of Ground Zero I felt a little surge of energy. I walked over to the Suburban and jumped in the back seat. I made sure I had my helmet and equipment. As I walked to the Suburban Rob caught up to me.

"Steve, I just heard. Rex died."

"Damn," I said. "What a place where dogs are even dying."

We piled into the Suburban and began the drive back to the Academy. I thought about what we have seen and felt, the debris field is a sea of rusted I-beams all labeled "4 tons." The smoke and dust permeated every bit of our clothing and the environment there.

I thought, "I do not want to ever come back here." I knew the body count would rise in time. I realized that this disaster will be ongoing, not a fixed number of deaths.

At the Academy I turned in my stuff and exchanged my uniforms and boots for new ones. I would have liked to keep them for personal reasons, but I knew they could not be healthy to wear.

The staff person said, "This crap is dirty, Boss, you don't want to keep that shit."

I asked, "What about my boots, they are pretty new."

"Give me everything, it is the least we can do for you guys. Not a problem Boss, a full set coming your way. Money is not an issue after this mess."

I felt like a rookie walking out with all new uniforms but I knew in my heart I had nothing to prove ever again. I would rather have clean uniforms and boots.

PART THREE
Putting the Pieces Together after 9/11

The World Trade Center will always cast a shadow over our minds for the rest of our lives. There is no getting over this one.

— FDNY Chief Daniel Nigro

XII
Life at Battalion 55 after 9/11

Return to Station.
Tuesday September 18, 2001

On Tuesday morning I reported back to my station Battalion 55. I arrived early because I had been waking up every 3 hours at night. I guessed I was still used to my hiking trips at Ground Zero. The station was empty and I started washing my turn out gear and my helmet. As I washed my helmet I smelled the dust from the pile and in my mind I saw the wreckage and rusted metal of Ground Zero. I thought, "What we have been through. Actually, what we will be going through for months."

EMT Kevin Enright arrived and greeted me saying, "Kanarian. Welcome back Lou."

I said, "Thanks."

Kevin continued, "Jesus, you were in the shit weren't you?"

"Yeah you could say that." I replied.

"What did you see?" Kevin asked.

I replied, "Not much to see brother, just a big mess."

Mike came over and said, "Welcome back, you the man boss."

I answered, "Good to see you Mike."

I fell into the routine of checking the radios, checking the schedule and getting units in service. I felt out of step and it felt weird sitting in an office with a chair and TV. I was admittedly out of step with the pace.

"Here you go Boss man," a nice cup of tea.

"Shit!" I thought to my self, "I haven't had tea at work since 9/11." The sweet tea felt good as I sipped and thought, "I am home again."

18 Charlie came into the station. "Where is Joe?" I asked.

The EMT driving 18 Charlie's truck exclaimed, "Are you kidding Lou?"

My heart sank as I expected to hear bad news.

The EMT continued, "Joe and Billy were nearly killed on 9/11! Those boys are out LODI." (LODI stands for Line of Duty Injury)

I asked, "What happened?"

He continued, "They ain't talking much but the gist of the story is they arrived at the World Trade Center and all Hell broke loose! When the Tower collapsed they got separated and buried. Billy was missing for days; Joe was buried in debris. Joe dug himself out from under a desk. He thought his partner was dead."

**Joe and Steve at Times Square after 9/11
(Photo Courtesy of Joe Conzo)**

"What happened to Billy," I asked.

"Turns out he was put on a ship and brought to Jersey. We all thought he was dead. He broke his tib fib (Tibia/Fibula). He will be out for a long time."

"Wow!" I thought, "I am glad they are ok. They aren't ok, but they are alive."

Captain Laurie Santo came in to the office and said, "Welcome back Steve. I am glad you're back safe."

I replied, "Thanks Captain."

She added, "I was at headquarters on 9/11 and we were tracking people down there. I had you on my list of people in USAR. I was keeping tabs on my flock."

I remarked, "Wow Captain, I did not think anyone even knew we were down there."

Laurie reiterated, "I was keeping an eye out for you guys."

I said, "Thanks Laurie."

Laurie added, "I am glad your back Steve. I am making soup and beef ribs today. I hope you brought your appetite."

I exclaimed, "Wow, sounds nice Laurie! Nice to be back home."

Captain Santo is a great leader. She leads from a perspective where people are important and she never gives up on anyone. I learned through time to adopt the "three strikes and your out" mantra of supervision. Laurie, however, does not give up on people at all. She operates from a religious basis and believes in people always, never giving up. I am grateful for having had such a caring boss who took interest in all of us at the station in the months following September 11, 2001. Captain Santo made an impossible time bearable.

Ralph Winburn walked into the office and greeted me saying, "Welcome back L-T. I heard you were in deep?"

I replied, "Yes, I was Pal. How did you make out that day?"

He answered, "I went to 49 and loaded in an ambulance with Matonis and Carlos' partner, and we drove into Manhattan. We were going to take the bridge but we were concerned the bridge was the next target, so we took the tunnel instead. Halfway through the tunnel, we all realized this was stupid because if this blows we were all going to be dead. I swear my heart did not beat until we reached daylight."

I spent the day doing tasks and getting re-acquainted with those colleagues I had last seen on 9/11.

As I prepared for the change of tour waiting for the Tour 3 lieutenant to arrive, I start closing out the radio log and looking over the Tour 3 Run Down.

I heard, "Hey Lou, welcome back."

I looked up and saw Booch, who I had not seen since September 11th.

I said, "I am glad to see you Booch. I am glad you are OK."

Keith McGregor walked in and turned his head quickly while

pulling down on his bullet proof vest to adjust it more comfortably. Before 9/11 the sight of a FDNY bulletproof vest seemed funny to me. Now the sight seemed somewhat more warranted given the changes in our world in the last two weeks.

Keith said, "Hey Lou, glad to see you, welcome back."

I stood up and shook both their hands and said, "The last time I saw you two guys things where chaotic."

Keith replied, "No Boss, they weren't chaotic. Things were pure unadulterated chaos."

I said, "You have such a way with words Keith."

"We work in chaotic situations on a daily basis, but September 11th was a war zone and pure chaos. It was like lava flowing from a volcano."

I inquired, "Booch I have to say that was some exchange on the phone. You have to take a shower? What was that all about buddy?"

Booch replied, "Boss, that shower probably saved my life."

I replied, "No doubt. When you left dude I did not know if I would ever see you or any of those guys on the ambulance again. I had such an empty feeling when you left the garage and turned right."

I asked, "Are your father and step-father ok?"

Booch replied, "Yup, they are fine. You would not believe what happened to us downtown. When we went to staging at Chelsea piers the captain would not let us go to the Trade Center. I told him we were Haz Tac personnel. We should be down there. We are trained to operate in that environment. I wanted to go downtown so bad. I grew up with a lot of those firefighters. "

Booch looked over at the poster on the wall and added, "I wanted to help rescue them. I cannot believe the boss downtown would not let us go down to the pile."

I said, "Booch, the Chief who was downtown did not want to put anyone else at risk. After the collapse of the Towers they did want to put any more people at risk. Plus there came a time when they realized they had enough ambulances and personnel to deal with the situation. After all there were only a handful of patients."

"Get this," Keith continued, "we are in staging for like 6 hours and the Captain would not let us go downtown. A bus of rookies from the Academy came and they were getting ready to go downtown. I said to Booch, this is bullshit, they are not going downtown before us."

Booch said, "I will handle this. I am the senior man here."

"Right," Keith added, "like he came out of the academy *three months* before me.

We all smiled.

Keith said, "A Gator ATV had rolled out with five of the sorriest looking people you've ever seen just covered with dust. The people looked like they were made of clay. They were covered with such powder, and there were patches of their bodies that were wet that had turned that gray dust to something like mud where they had been crying. They were all crusty and cakey. It was *everywhere*! They would shake their head and their hair would look like a paint brush. They looked like they just walked out of Hell.

We walked up to one of them and said, "Do you need anything?" and handed him a bottle of water.

He said, "Yeah, just help me get this stuff off."

So we started taking their things off the Gator and washing them with water.

Booch interjected, "As the crew got off the Cushman the rookies put their tech bags on the Gator. I walked up and knocked off their brand spanking new bags and I told them 'If anyone is going to the pile it is us. We are senior here.' We got on the Gator and drove down West Street."

Keith said, "When we got Downtown we were stopped by a Lieutenant who told us he needed one EMT. I told Booch, You're the senior man, go with the Lieutenant."

Booch said, "They sent me to the Treatment area. We sat around and did dick. I needed to make sure my father and step-father were ok, and they had *me* in Treatment."

I responded, "Booch I respect you for that. That must have been hard. But you did what you were supposed to do. You did your job. We cannot have everybody running round doing their own thing."

"I know boss. I know. Tell you one thing. I am glad that I was not in that Fire Academy Class that graduated last week. I would be dead right now," Booch replied.

"Maybe not, Booch," I answered.

Booch responded saying, "No. My Dad would have pulled strings to get me to where I wanted to go. I would have been downtown. I would have been up in the Towers."

"Booch, sometimes one decision breaks a bigger cross we cannot even anticipate," I replied.

"Your right Boss. Sure are right about that," Booch said and then added, "Many of those firefighters who died it was their first day on the rear step."

Keith interjected, "Let's go Booch, "Time to go save lives."

"Stay safe," I remarked.

Keith replied, "Always. Nice to have you back boss."

My first day back at work felt weird, but I was getting back in the groove. It was good to see people I knew. My relief came in and took over the station duties. We exchanged some pertinent information about units and personnel and I headed home.

Late that night I woke up and was wide-awake after two hours of sleep. I went to the window to see what was going on outside. As I looked out the window into my backyard, I saw the burned out remains of Number 5 World Trade Center.

Burned Out Remains of Number 5 World Trade Center

"What the..?" I thought.

"Am I dreaming? Is this a flashback?"

I turned my head and saw the wallpaper. I pinched my arm, and thought, *"No. I am awake!"*

I closed my eyes and looked again. The visual image of Number 5 World Trade Center was so vibrant on my mind I saw it with my eyes open. I thought, "I have got to get some rest." My body was used to being up all night and working full out.

"Signal 5-5-5-5... The Chief of Department Regrets … "

I was driving my patrol vehicle West back to my area and I heard an alert tone, "Beeeep, Beeep. Beep. "All units standby for a department wide announcement. Signal 5-5-5-5 has been transmitted. The Chief of Department regrets to announce the passing of the following members of the department. Firefighter..." The dispatcher continued by stating the name of each firefighter found, his rank and the fact that they succumbed to injuries sustained on September 11, 2001 at the World Trade Center. Lately this was the norm. The announcements of death had been coming regularly, two or three a day as they found bodies deep in the pit. *The fact that several firefighters, Hell, a whole fire company had been lost was unbelievable.*

In the history of the FDNY, firemen had died in the line of duty at MCIs but this loss was of a greater magnitude. In one morning 343 firefighters were taken by terrorism. As they called the names of the firefighters and their grade, I looked to my left and felt the warm sunlight on my face. The warmth felt good. I looked at the ground while the dispatcher repeated the message again. I looked at the asphalt and the voice drifted off.

As I felt the sunlight and warmth I looked at the street and noticed the white speckles among the asphalt. I then noticed a small green piece of green glass. As the clouds shifted the speckles of glass twinkled. I was sitting and staring at the ground for what felt like a few minutes. I could not say I was thinking of any one thing more than I was just existing, looking at the detail in the asphalt and enjoying the warmth of the sun.

An Angel Named Abuela

"Poppy, scuuz, poppy!" I became aware of a voice calling someone. "Poppy, Bomberos! Mila!" I looked to my left and saw an elderly Hispanic woman who was pushing a wire laundry basket with her groceries. "Mila. Poppy." She made the sign of the cross and blew me a kiss. She reminded me of my grandmother. I smiled and nodded. I was in such a deep relaxing mode I began driving slowly down the road watching the Abuela in my rear view mirror. I thought about how a woman who I had never met stopped and showed such caring to me. She may have been a person who would have been pissed off with our siren or our truck blocking her car in the past. Now she felt absolute love and empathy.

"Condition 5-5 Send It Over..."

Then I heard, "I need a unit for a pedestrian struck. Any units near Southern Boulevard and E 180?"

I answered, "Condition 5–5 send it over, 18B I'm blocks away."

"Roger, 18B and Condition five-five you got it."

I sat upright and pushed the accelerator smoothly increasing speed. The faster I drove the peripheral scene became a blur. I tuned the corner and saw pandemonium in the street. I saw a man waving both arms intently to get my attention then signaling, "come here with one arm." This is the gesture I call the cardiac arrest wave. I pulled up to the scene and saw a patient with deformed upper legs who was awake and breathing. To save time I grabbed the long board and collar from the back of the truck.

As I approached the patient I saw the deformity in the upper legs that kind of deformity that tells you, *this is fractured*, this is no rule out fracture, this femur is broken. The patient had already started becoming pale and sweaty. I could see the lips were pale, which is a sign of decompensated shock.

"Time to skidoo Steve," I thought. I placed the cervical collar on the patient and asked him his name. He responded, "Juan, Juan Ramirez."

I said, "Juan, hang in there, brother. We are on the way to Jacobi. We are going to take good care of you."

I motioned to the bystanders and said, "You grab the hips; you grab the chest from the side. On the count of three. One, two, three," we rolled the man in unison and slid the board behinds him. I felt his back for deformity and bleeding, none noted, no weapons either, that is a good thing.

I could hear the diesel engine of an ambulance bearing down to the scene. I steadied the patient's head and pushed the mic on the radio and said, "Hands Conzo, hands only." Soon there after the crowd parted and Conzo and his partner were there to help.

"Give me that strap sir," Conzo quipped, 1, 2, 3."

The patient was strapped, his head taped to the backboard and we were on the way to the bus. I lifted the patient up to Billy and said, "Jacobi brother! Medics, none. Don't need them. He needs a surgeon." I closed the door and as the bus began rolling to the hospital I thought, "Wow that was fun! A good job makes a difference. A shame it went so fast."

We essentially have 10 minutes on the scene. We call it the platinum 10 minutes. Surgeons need to get the patient from the scene to surgery in one hour. They call it the golden hour.

I pulled off my blue gloves and returned to the Conditions car. I began driving to Jacobi behind the BLS unit. They were driving efficiently but smoothly.

Billy called in a trauma note to the dispatcher. "Notify Jacobi we are coming in with a 20 year old male bilateral femur fractures, no LOC (loss of consciousness), BP (blood pressure) 96 by palpation, pulse 130 and resps 28, we will be there in 7 minutes."

As we drove I realized how lucky we are to have 2 trauma centers in the Bronx both in 15-minutes from the scene. In some parts of the country medics have to fly at high speed to try to reach a trauma center within the golden hour. 18B backed into the emergency room and several EMTs and medics came to help unload the patient.

A sea of people surrounded the patient as he was pushed inside the trauma room, someone said, "20 year old male, struck by an auto, no LOC, significant mechanism on the car, windshield was spidery.

Has deformity to both femurs, crepitus on pelvis and decreased breath sounds on the right."

Dr. Lombardi ordered the residents to "Put in chest tubes, paralyze the patient and secure a tube." He turned to the radiologist and ordered, "Chest, pelvis cervical spine lateral x-rays."

A lab technician reported, "Jimmy, yup, the patient with the stab to the belly is positive hemocult." (Test showed blood in stool).

"Ok, call surgery get him up there ASAP, Jimmy, yes, the pulmonary edema patient it or is? 200 over 120 resps are 36 good. IV (intravenous) nitro drip increase to till she opens up."

"Hi Doc, how are you? I asked.

He answered, "Busy. Busy."

"This is like an auto shop," I said smiling. "Cardiac in 1, trauma in 7, fender in 3." Walking briskly I asked, "What are you doing?"

Dr. Lombardi answered, "I have to check on a patient in the chamber. Be right back."

Dr. Lombardi was the director of the ED here at Jacobi. He had been an ambulance driver and EMT and then he was in the first class of paramedics in the city. Dr. Lombardi is a living legend.

Jacobi is the only center for hyperbaric medicine. Hyperbaric chambers are used for treatment of decompression illness and carbon monoxide (CO) inhalation. A patient who has inhaled carbon monoxide will not be able to carry oxygen to the cells, CO is 220 times more attracted to hemoglobin than oxygen. A non-rebreather with oxygen will take hours to blow off the CO. Put them in the chamber and they are clear in 40 minutes.

Doctor Lombardi returns and I asked, "Doc, how do you keep up with the cases. You see pulmonary edema, trauma, burns and snake bites. How do you keep up on everything?"

He responded, "I read."

Dr. Lombardi walked over to trauma to check on the suturing of a man who put his arm through a plate glass window.

"What do you mean you read?" I asked Dr. Lombardi.

He turned and took papers from his back pocket. "Steve, I tear out articles on topics I need to know, articles by Docs I follow. I read at a red light. I read in the bathroom and I read while waiting for bloods."

I nodded my head as Dr. Lombardi walked back to the trauma room. I thought, "That is a professional, continually learning and wanting the best for his patients."

I felt wary now that the adrenaline was wearing off, the patient was going up to surgery with a decent BP. It looks like he was going to survive. Time to go home.

Caring for Our Own

An ambulance comes in "hot" with lights flashing and a sense of urgency. I thought, "This must be something good. The crew is bringing in a cardiac arrest." I gave a hand unloading the patient from the ambulance and moving the stretcher into the hospital. A paramedic is doing great CPR. The other medic jumps down from the ambulance with his paperwork and ribbons of ECG tape to document the arrest and show the hospital staff.

He reported, "I gave another epi as we pulled in, we are up to date, tube is in with equal breath sounds."

"Hey Lou," a familiar voice rang out from the end of the ambulance bay. I can't quite place the voice but it is familiar.

I turn around and see Kevin Cassidy zipping over towards me in his usual "high energy" state. Kevin Cassidy is a medic that I knew from my days working evening on the West Side of the Bronx. Kevin used to back my partner and me up on calls when he was an EMT. In the late 1980s we did a lot of serious jobs with fewer ambulances. Everybody was closer in those days.

I thought back to the day we met. Kevin and I were doing CPR on an elderly male on Marion Avenue. I noticed Kevin's professionalism and attention to detail. He took the job seriously. His zeal to do a good job was a welcome breath of fresh air from the minimalism often seen in the city.

"Hey what is your name," I inquired.

"Kevin. Kevin Cassidy," he replied.

I said, "You're awesome Kevin, keep up those good compressions."

I kneeled down and found the IV tubing injection port. Pushing the epinephrine into the injection port I looked up at Kevin and asked, "What are you doing after work?"

"Nothing really," he replied.

I said, "I think you should meet us for drinks later. We can all hang out at Rhodes. What do you think, Don?"

My partner answered, "Sounds like a plan. He is a good man."

"Sounds good," Kevin responded. I could see the pride he felt in being included as part of the team. That day right there on the floor of a dying man, while he compressed the patient's chest, a lifelong brotherhood was forged.

I walked toward him and we exchanged a handshake and a warm welcome. Kevin looked fit and trim, chewing his tobacco, bouncing from one foot to the other while straining to stand still. Kevin is so energetic I often believe that his veins are filled with epinephrine. We once gave him a pendant with an ampule of 1:1,000 epinephrine labeled, "Essence of Kevin."

Kevin is a man of action. I am a more a reflective person. That is why we made a good team.

"How are you doing Kevin?" I inquired.

"Great. How have you been brother?" Kevin inquired in return.

I told him, "Honestly Kevin, I am dragging. I have trouble sleeping and have zero energy."

Kevin replied, "I know how you feel brother. 9/11 is really weighing heavy on all of us. I can't imagine what it was like down there. I wish I could have gotten down there."

As Kevin talked he used his hands to gesture and bounced from one foot to the other.

He added, "My Captain held us back at the station because he felt Tour 3 was more important."

I responded, "I can see you feel bad, but Kevin, there was not much to do down there, except take risks and get exposed."

Kevin changed the subject saying, "That sure was some day. I was awakened by fighter jets circling over my house."

"What did you say?" I inquired.

He said, "Didn't I tell you?"

I replied, "No, we really have not spoken since that day."

Kevin answered, "I had done overtime the night before and went home to sleep. I was awakened by jets flying over my house. The first time I thought it was a freak thing." He paused to spit some chewing tobacco into a cup and continued saying, "I went out to my patio and saw two F–14s fly over my head. Steve, these were not the ones that you see at air shows. These planes had no markings and were loaded down with weapons — you know, missiles. These planes looked angry and they were moving with afterburners on. It was about 9:30 in the morning."

I exclaimed, "Kevin, I never heard you say that before, that must have been something."

I thought about the images Kevin must have seen, F–14s roaring over Van Courtland Park, circling the city looking for targets in the wake of the South Tower collapsing. Imagine the mindset of pilots scrambling off of a carrier somewhere in the Atlantic and flying to Manhattan to protect the city.

I imagined that they were flying in to the city thinking of how they might have to shoot down a civilian airliner. I wondered if they knew the target. I wondered if the pilots were conditioned to disregard the target. No, I can't imagine an American fighter pilot that would not be bothered for the rest of his life having shot down an airliner filled with civilians, then wondering if it was necessary.

But here, now, I figured they would have been wishing they had been in place in time to take out the airliners as the two most iconic buildings of international relations and business lay collapsed in the street and thousands of people were missing. That is real anger and the kind of regret that will last a lifetime. As I thought about the pilots and the victims, tears welled up in my eyes and my chin quivered.

"That must have been something Kevin," I responded.

"Yeah, that shit was off the hook, Steve. So, here I was in my shorts out on the patio and my phone was ringing off the hook. I answered the phone and my mother asked, 'are you alright?' I reassured her saying, Yeah, Mom I am fine. I was sleeping in bed. I then realized I had eight messages from people calling to see if I was home or downtown. I went into work and loaded my equipment on a bus to go downtown with another medic, but we were stopped because the Captain was concerned about running units in the evening shift. I really wanted to get down there and help. There was no other place to be for me."

"I am sorry you did not get to go down there," I replied.

Kevin reported that, "On that Wednesday the union sent out a page for members of the service (MOS) that needed help in New Jersey Hospitals. Apparently some of the EMTs we thought were dead had been taken to Jersey in ferries. I jumped up and called the Local 2507 and told them I live in Jersey and I would be glad to help MOS in the hospital. I went to one hospital and saw a medic going home who had no clothes. He was going to be dropped off at the bridge and try to get a Conditions boss to pick him up. I found him some clothes and gave him a ride home, to his door."

I added, "I know you wanted to go downtown Kevin but I am telling you, there was nothing good going on down there. Plus you made a difference taking jobs and keeping the Service running in the Bronx."

Kevin replied, "Yeah, I guess your right. Good to see you."

I said, "Brother, yeah, you too Kevin, take care. Good to talk to you. Now go 98!"

We both laughed, knowing that I cannot be hard on such a good old friend and that Kevin does not need to be told what to do. Kevin is among the best of NYC EMS.

I leaned back on the brick wall outside the ER and closed my eyes in the sunlight. Even though it was chilly out, the sun felt warm. I felt the wall on my hands as I leaned against the brick wall. Our team would gather here in the 1980s after doing calls. We would reflect on our calls decide what we did well and what we could have done better. We complained about the bad bosses and partners that irritated us. This wall was a gathering place to rest and regroup, in solitude away from the craziness of the streets in the summer.

I realized how ironic it was that some of the bosses have complained about all of their people, but the events of 9/11 reminded us that in the end we are all people trying to make a living and trying to make a difference.

I thought, "We must remember not to let the petty differences get in the way of the big picture."

As a medic I learned that every day you wake up is a good

day, because some people don't wake up ever again. We have to remember to honor and appreciate each other and try not to let the daily annoyances and stressors eat each other up.

I thought, "This wall was a special place in the day."

I smiled thinking of the great medics I have worked with as well as the medics who were characters who would have no problem listening to the big game on AM radio while others did their jobs. I thought about the EMTs that are no longer with us because they were killed riding their bike to work or died in the Trade Center as firefighters.

I was glad to know that there are places in the world that have not changed after all that has taken place. I saw ambulances pulling in the ER bay and some leaving like the tidal flow that continues year after year, unaffected by hurricanes.

It is funny how we meet paramedics and EMTs under dire circumstances and build bonds on our jobs that last forever. I may not see someone for months; then we pick up the phone or meet in the ER and talk for a long time, like it was yesterday we worked together. That is not friendship. That is brotherhood!

XIII
The 300-Pound Bear in the Room

Baltimore Bound. October 2001

My cell phone was ringing. "Hello," I answered.

"Hey Buddy. Glad to hear your voice," Jason said, "I am glad you are ok. I was concerned when I could not reach you on 9/11."

"Thanks Buddy. What's up?" I asked, changing the subject to avoid the uncomfortable feeling that comes when men show emotion.

"I know we had invited you down to Baltimore to speak at the refresher course. If you don't feel up to it I understand," Jason replied.

"No. I am fine and looking forward to the presentation now more than ever. I have some great photos and lessons learned," I said.

He answered, "Ok, I am glad you want to come down. If you have second thoughts let me know. It would not be a problem. I know how rough something like you've been through can be."

I replied, "No Jason. I am a man of my word I will be there."

I thought, "I have spent a life of being dependable and doing a job until it is done. I do not have a problem lecturing to a refresher class of medics."

"Ok see you tomorrow," Jason responded, "stop by the college and I will introduce you to the staff at the college.

"Will do Jason," I quipped.

Driving down to Baltimore I had a lot of time to think and see the sights. I had brought dozens of FDNY shirts to sell to raise money for a fund in honor of the firemen and policemen who died on 9/11.

I swerved my car and jammed on the brakes. "Jes-us. Watch it mister! What a reckless driver," I thought.

The drive to Baltimore was a nice opportunity to get away and see something different. Work has been tense and there has been a lot of arguing. I turned off the exit and went right.

I thought, "Shoot, wrong way." I turn around in a driveway and saw a car almost hit me.

"Watch it will you." I murmured. "That is twice today," I thought and added, "Jerks!"

When I arrived at Jason's College I walked down the hall and met a staff member. I said, "I am looking for Jason Hums."

"You must be Jason's friend from New York," he said.

I thought, "How does he know that?

"How do you know?" I asked.

He replied, "You have that dark cloud of doom and gloom over your head."

"No. I am fine," I said reassuringly.

"Sure you are," he quipped.

I heard, "Hey Buddy!" as Jason greeted me as he emerged from his office and added, "Let's go get some lunch and we will get to class in time for your lecture."

"Sounds good! I had a dangerous trip down here. Got cut off twice. Close calls." I said.

Jason stopped, turned to me and asked, "Are you ok? You guys have been through a lot."

"I am fine Jason. I am proud. I did everything I was asked to do. Never gave up; never backed down." I stated.

"Ok, let's go." Jason answered.

As we drove to the classroom, I jumped and yelled, "Watch out, pointing to a car coming in from the other lane."

"I saw him, Steve," Jason said and then asked, "How are Moira and the kids?"

"An obvious attempt to change the subject," I thought and then responded, "They are good. I have been working a lot and Moira has been picking up the slack. She is very supportive."

We pulled into the Harbor Plaza and began walking to the sports restaurant. Jason pointed to an office building and said, "This is our Trade Center. When the attack occurred people thought this Trade Center was attacked. I knew it was New York City. I knew they were back."

I replied, "That small building?"

"Yup, people react to what they know," Jason answered.

I heard, "Craaa-sh!" Suddenly the sound of metal crashing and grinding against concrete filled the air. I ducked down to one knee and braced myself, squinting with my head lowered waiting for the impact of what the hell that noise was. A skate boarder skirted by us and looked me over without noticing. The skater casually pushed with his right leg a few times before rolling off into the parking lot.

Jason helped me up and said, "No, you're not stressed."

We both smiled. My smile was half turned. Jason's smile was that of a concerned friend who knew about PTSD and traumatic stress.

Having been a medic in the Bronx for many years, I have seen a lot of really bad calls. I had been to hundreds of cardiac arrests, dozens of multiple shootings and some severe assaults. I had even been at the largest homicide in US history, the Happy Land Fire.

I thought, "Why was this incident different? I have never been bothered by PTSD. Cumulative stress was a different story, but not PTSD. The worst I had experienced is stress for a few days that dissipated with time and rest. I was thinking, "How does Jason know? What does he see that I do not feel?"

As we ate lunch Jason talked about stress and his role in a peer counseling team. I began feeling like the patient and not the rescuer and said, "No really, I am fine. I will be fine. I have always dealt with things on my own."

We drove to the firehouse to give the mass casualty management (MCI) lecture to refresher students from around the country. I was a little nervous about speaking cold to an unknown crowd but I knew I could do this. While lecturing I pointed out problems with MCI management like lack of triage, failure to sort patients after triage and the fact that we often overload one hospital. I pointed out that after 9/11 St. Vincent's Hospital in downtown Manhattan was overwhelmed by walking wounded and people driven there by private vehicles, taxis and police cars.

The lecture continued and we joked and laughed. I set them up to play a joke on a good friend of mine, Mike, who was lecturing later in the evening. I said, "When Mike goes to speak, keep interrupting him, ask him if he knows Steve Kanarian. Keep chopping him up. Did you work with Steve? He is the man."

They all laughed and agreed to play the prank as we continued with the lecture.

I was lecturing on my "Safety Rules to Live By and Stay Alive By." (see Appendix) As I talked about the safety rules I began to feel anxious and my mind drifted to the World Trade Center rescue efforts and the sights I saw. I started thinking of the pile, the smell of dust and the smoke. I could hear the chatter of the jackhammers and engines of the front loaders.

I struggled to focus on the lecture. Soon I got to the rule about staging and said, "Ark your vehicles two to three times the height of the building to avoid being crushed in a collapse."

Suddenly, I heard an unrecognizable voice outside of me blurt out, "Save the people from the building. We have to get them out!"

In an effort to keep speaking and gloss over whatever the Hell that outburst was, I pressed the "Return" key on my laptop and up flashes a photo of a fire truck with the American flag on it. I thought, "Premature. This was meant for the end of my lecture. I must have hit the 'End' key rather than the return key. Idiot!"

I stood there cold and trembling. My chest was numb but I could feel my pulse bounding in my carotid arteries. Time passed. I do not know how long.

Jason came up front and asked, "Are you ok?

I shook my head, "No."

Jason announced, "Ladies and Gentlemen, let's take a break. Take a 20-minute break."

"Let's get some water, Steve," he added.

We went to an instructor's room and I drank some cold water and apologized to Jason.

"I don't know what happened," I said.

"You had an intrusive thought, a flashback," Jason informed me.

I was now aware my chest and back were soaked with sweat. I breathed deeply and got my focus back.

"It is no wonder you are stressed after what you lived through. This is normal. You would be abnormal if 9/11 did not bother you. When those Towers fell, I remembered working at Beekman. I felt that I had to be at the Trade Center. I was there in 1993. I felt guilty for being alive," Jason shared.

I finished the lecture in an uncomfortable and choppy manner but got the objectives across. The class stood up and clapped their hands thanking me for sharing my experience and lessons on MCI management.

Driving back to New York the next day I thought about the incidents with the cars on the way down and how I overreacted. I remembered this being called a startle response when you are under severe stress. I thought about the skate boarder that made me dive for the ground and the incident with the fire truck and my shouting out during the lecture.

My thoughts returned back to work where employees were arguing with each other and with bosses. Bosses were arguing with dispatchers and other bosses. "Jesus!" I thought, "We are all stressed out and nobody realizes it because the whole city is stoked to the maximum with PTSD."

I recalled a story of how the task force members who went to Oklahoma City in 1993 and said when they were working in the basement and they were working fast and hard, they mentioned they should take a break or slow down. The team wanted to find patents on their Tour and make a difference, so they continued to dig and search, dig and search. Suddenly, there was complete quiet and the cold smell of dirt filled the air. No noise, they laid in the dirt wondering if they were dead, victims of a secondary collapse.

A voice spoke, "Hold on guys, shit I think I pulled a plug out by accident."

Soon the generator and lights came back on. The team working in the basement of the Murrah Federal Building had realized they had overextended themselves. They all agreed to back out and take a rest, refocus and gain perspective. During the effort to save lives and make a difference, they had become affected by tunnel vision. These were highly experienced rescuers with the best training.

I was surprised that even trained personnel would not realize they had overextended themselves. During hazardous material training we were taught to calibrate an instrument in a "Clean" environment. In other words if you're looking for Hydrogen Sulfide in a confined space you should calibrate the instrument street side. The Oklahoma City incident showed me that you have to step outside an incident to gain a clear perspective.

What was amazing about the World Trade Center Attack is I had to go to Baltimore to realize I *was* affected by PTSD. I drove back to the city with the perspective that our whole department and city was affected by stress in the wake of September 11, 2001. I promised to keep that thought in my mind and help mend fences between employees and look out for our employees when I went back to work in the city.

Work Overload and Stress.
February 2002

I was beginning to realize how bad things were getting. Even after realizing there was a lot of stress in the city I found myself getting short-tempered at work and frustrated. Unfortunately, we gave our all at work and saved very little for our families. I found myself yelling at my wife and kids. I did not mean to be short-tempered, but it was hard to control.

We worked hard and then some. We worked overtime and did not get enough sleep. How were we to recover from such an event when the 911 System kept running, and now we had a huge effort at Ground Zero to find the remains of thousands of people, coworkers, and some friends? I tried avoiding confrontation and going with the flow. It worked some of the time, but tempers would flare. Still, we tried to get the job done.

After hearing some EMTs had got time off from FEMA for stress, I called and asked for time off from the Counseling Unit. I was told, "Lieutenant, we have hundreds who are much more worse off than you. Some firehouses lost twenty firefighters. We cannot give you time off."

I wondered, "How the Hell do EMTs get time off and I can't?" I realized they must have said the magic words to pose a threat to themselves. Most of us kept carrying the burden, forcing a smile and doing our job.

My son's first birthday was in February. I had trouble focusing on his birthday when he was born last year. I could not think of a link to connect Michael's birthday to. Now I will never forget his birthday. Michael was born on February 11, 2001, seven months before 9/11.

I tried to be tolerant of my children and not explode but it was impossible. I would find a slight distraction would make me drop a glass in the kitchen. When Captain Santo asked me how I was sleeping I replied, "Great, I get three hours every night."

Although I knew there was a problem, I did not want to be the one to back down and go for "help." We were the help, the ones people looked up to in their worst moments of life. I found myself driving at extremely high speeds to work to feel something. Life felt like I was distant, in an amniotic sac, unaffected by emotion.

I once told my friend, Kevin, that he should get a bite to eat while he waited for us. He replied, "I am not hungry." I quipped, "What does being hungry have to do with eating."

Now I was not eating all of my meals and leaving food on the plate. Something was very wrong but I kept going to work and doing my job. I felt the need to release these emotions. I would sit in my chair at home and try to let go, nothing would happen. I once pulled alongside the highway in a rest area and tried to shed a tear. Nothing would happen. No release.

Keith Working at "The Pit"

Keith walked into the office and said, "Good morning Lou. I am here for a mutual for Kenny."

"You look tired Keith," I said.

He answered, "I am Boss. I have been pulling insane overtime at Ground Zero.

167

I asked, "Anything good happening down there? Have they found Carlos Lillo yet? Do they even know where he is?"

"No, not yet," he responded and added "Boss, I have had enough of working downtown lately. It's time to take a break."

"Had enough Keith?" I inquired.

He explained:

> It is hard to feel anything about it because everyday it just eats at you that much more. It was an amazing thing to see how much the will can overcome your physical limitations just by sheer want. Recently Ground Zero is being called "the pit."

> Looking for the remains was crazy to see because it had gotten to the point where you couldn't even tell what was human or what was debris. We had a small bulldozer pick up something at a huge pile, drive a little bit away from where the guys were standing and then it would start to back out slowly and shake out the bucket and laying out debris into a long swath or strip. Then 10 or so fireman would break off the strips with large rakes and start raking out all the debris to sift through. All the debris, most of the debris, in the pit was literally sifted through piece by piece.

I interrupted him and said, "That's amazing! It would seem impossible to go through all that debris."

Keith explained:

> "Yeah, it was! You just couldn't understand it unless you saw it. At that point they had set up a mask unit, a respirator unit, right next to what we called the Taj Mahal that was like an oasis in the desert because there was this huge dome where you would have a shower. There was a tunnel that you would walk through to hose or vacuum the dust to clean yourself off before you could go inside to use the bathroom and get some water. Right next to the Taj Mahal, they had a mini cafeteria set up so the shift guys could take a few minutes to recover.

When they found someone, they would call for a Gator to go down to the pit. We'd go down to the pile to pick up the remains and see the firefighters reaching down and picking up debris and asking through the mask questions like, "Hey you know, what do you think? What do you think; is this plastic or what?" The only way they could find out if it was actually human remains was to pull the mask up over their faces and smell it. Then they'd go, "Yeah this is human remains," throw it in a little red bag and wave over somebody or call on a radio. Then another firefighter or somebody else in a Gator would roll over to them with a GPS unit and mark the exact spot where they found the remains, tag it and document where it came from. The little remains were collected on a Gator and shipped up to the morgue where they were dropped off.

The ambulances and EMS personnel were utilized most when we got a call for "significant remains." When there was a call to respond to a report for significant remains, we would go down and there would be a bunch of people standing in the pile. We would pick up the body, the significant remains, which was probably just a torso or a leg or a hip and arm or the remains of a bunker coat or a crushed helmet that was something of some significance — not just bits of debris. You could actually identify it as a part of a human being.

We would pick up the remains, place it on a stokes stretcher and then go to some sort of chapel in there. It didn't matter what the denomination was, nobody cared, as long as it was a chapel. Somebody in there would say a prayer. We all would bow our heads and take off our helmets. Then we'd walk the remains up the ramp or put the remains on the Gator and drive the Gator up the ramp to where the ambulance was backed into the top of the ramp. We would load the remains that had an American Flag draped over it into the back of the ambulance. Then the ambulance would then take the remains to the city morgue.

At that point Keith reiterated, "I have had enough!"

I exclaimed, "It sounds like you have had *more than enough*! I was sure I did not want to go down there again when I left the second week. Let's take a break. There are some people here to thank you for what you've done, Keith."

Brothers from Maine Showing Support

Kevin Bachi and I started our careers as paramedics together in paramedic class at Northeastern University. Kevin was eager to move to New York City and convinced me to join him in the Bronx. Ironically, Kevin returned to Maine and I stayed on in New York City. Despite the distance we maintained our friendship through a burning desire to make a difference. When Kevin needed help putting a roof on his barn in the Winter, I was glad to go help him. On September 11, 2001 Kevin watched the towers collapse on TV and when he was unable to reach his old partners and me on the phone he started packing to come to Ground Zero to find us. Luckily, he was able to reach us when cell phone service was restored. This is the kind of bond we share. I visit him often, so he knows I *love* Maine lobster.

Kevin and the fire fighters from his station were going to visit Ground Zero, and they decided to surprise everyone at our station with a special treat for lunch. I was happy Kevin was coming for a visit and was in the office awaiting their arrival.

Keith walks into the office and said, "Good morning Lou. I am here for a mutual for Kenny."

"You look tired Keith," I said.

He answered, "I am boss. I have been pulling insane overtime at Ground Zero. Anything good happening down there? Have they found Carlos Lillo yet? Do they even know where he is?"

"No, not yet," I responded.

McGregor called me saying, "Lou, there are guys to see you at the back door. They look like firemen, but they are not from around here."

"Alright!" I exclaimed, "They are here. Let's go help them."

We helped Kevin bring in boxes of food and bags of fresh corn.

"What do you guys have?" Keith asked.

My friend Kevin replied, "We have a tribute for you fine men and women fresh from Maine."

Kevin lifted the cover off the box and brushed the ice to the side exposing live, uncooked lobsters.

"Awesome." Keith exclaimed.

I said, "That is your surprise today for lunch. Let the units know to come back around 1 pm for dinner. My good Friend Kevin Bachi and his buddies from Kennebunk Maine are on their way to Ground Zero and stopped here to make lunch for you guys."

John came into the kitchen and asked, "What's for lunch?"

"What would you expect from Maine?" I asked.

"Lobsta" John said, with his Long Island accent and then added, "But that is out of the question. Too expensive."

"Really. Who is the man, McGregor?" I quipped.

"You are Lou," he acknowledged.

I said, "We have lobster dinner for everybody on duty today."

"You are the man, Lou," McGregor stated.

I greeted my friend saying, "Hey Kevin. Glad you could make it."

"I promised I would be here, right? Did you doubt me at all?" Kevin asked.

"Nope! I did not," I said emphatically.

"Guys, set up the pans and get to work, I ordered. Then I asked Kevin, "Do you guys need anything?"

He replied, "Steve, just stand back we have it all in hand. Bear and the guys will take care of everything."

"Fine, let me show you around," I offered. Kevin and I walked upstairs to the apparatus floor and looked around.

Kevin said, "I tried reaching Pete Kearney. I can't get in touch with him."

I replied, "I know Kevin. I left messages myself. He must be doing massive overtime. I am sorry. I know you were hoping to ride along with him or pay him a visit."

"No problem, something will work out when we go downtown," Kevin said.

We sat down and enjoyed "lobsta", potatoes and corn — courtesy of the Kennebunk Fire Department. The guys were flabbergasted and enjoyed the meal.

Kevin spoke to the guys at the table saying, "We watched 9/11 on TV and wished we could have been here to help our brothers in the field. We respect and appreciate what you guys did. This is a token of our appreciation after what you guys have been through. Remember, you are not alone. Now eat your lobster!"

Keith and a couple of others said, "Thank you."

Kevin replied, "No problem. We have your back."

"Thank you Kevin. I will meet you at Ground Zero after work tonight," I said.

He responded, "Ok Brother! See you then."

After work, I drove to Ground Zero to meet with Kevin and his guys, but they were nowhere to be found. I inquired in Engine 10 Ladder 10 and was told, "The guys with the lobster? They are awesome. They are around somewhere."

As I walked and spoke to coworkers assigned downtown, I heard the roar of a fire engine straining to climb the grade from Ground Zero. Squad 61 was raised from the pit like a phoenix over a war zone with an American flag on the rear step and firemen hanging on everywhere, including some grinning firefighters from Maine.

Kevin exclaimed, "Steve, you will never guess what happened. We came downtown and Pete and his crew were here tonight. They gave us a ride to the pit and we helped with debris removal."

Kevin jumped off Squad 61 and I said, "Hello," to Pete.

Pete was on the only Special Operations Command Squad that survived on September 11th. Pete told me that his lieutenants refused to go downtown until they were dispatched. As noted above, one of the tenets on MCI management is that there is no freelancing, no one man shows. The adherence to this tenet on the part of Squad 61 made them the only SOC unit, squad or rescue to survive.

Pete is one of my good September 11th stories. When I saw him I was grateful and realized he could have been number 344.

"Sorry I did not answer your calls. We have been super busy," Pete said apologetically.

"No problem, Pete," I replied.

I added, "What a freak thing meeting up down here."

"No brother, fate!" Pete said.

Kevin and I looked over toward each other and grinned. What a deal, bumping into Pete at Ground Zero when he worked in the Bronx.

One of the firefighters came over to talk to Kevin and pointed at the equipment. A few of them gathered around and chatted quietly. The expression on their face was one of being impressed and in awe. They separated and went back toward the squad.

Kevin walked back toward me and faced Ground Zero. "What is up Kevin?" I inquired.

He replied, "Steve, where we come from if a guy is talking shit about working hard we can tell that he is full of shit when we drive by his house and see his backhoe covered in rust. These front loaders and excavators are some of the biggest produced. They do not have a spot of rust and they are worn thin. The only way to do that is work like hell 24 hours a day in a place like Ground Zero. To my guys that says it all."

"People are taught to talk to others in the terms the audience can understand. I guess people interpret things differently. I never would have thought about the trucks being worn out," I said toward Kevin who was watching the machines go back and forth carrying metal, dumping the metal and then relaying metal to the next loader that dumps the metal into the waiting dump truck. Kevin's trance was broken by the sound of water spraying the metal and washing off the dust-covered steel.

Kevin replied, "That's right brother, all politics is local."

**Kevin Viewing Ground Zero from the
Engine 10 Ladder 10 House Roof**

Kevin and I went to the Engine 10 Ladder 10 House and walked to the rear stairs leading to the roof. As we walked to the edge of the roof, the entire Ground Zero panorama unfolded and Kevin and I stopped chatting and looked over the sight before us.

I said, "Kevin those boxes you see are the I-beams that separated each floor. The material that is jammed in there is the contents of the floors above — people, equipment and debris. Firemen and policemen alike."

Then Kevin was emotional and said, "You know Steve, when I could not reach you and Carl I was packing my bags to come down here. I thought you guys were gone."

I thought about what Kevin was saying. It is not often one man shares with another the depth of their relationship. I appreciated his candor and the fact that if something happened to me, he would step in and help out.

"Thanks, brother! I appreciate it," I replied.

PART FOUR
Dealing with 343 Deaths, Sadness and Anger

There is a sacredness in tears. They are not the mark of weakness, but of power.

They speak more eloquently than ten thousand tongues. They are messengers of overwhelming grief ... and unspeakable love.
— *Washington Irving*

XIV
Road to Getting Help.

"You're Lucky to Be Alive!"

One day at work, I found myself looking at the faces of the 343 FDNY members who died on September 11, 2001. As I looked at the pictures, I could see the innocence in their faces. I shook my head and said a short prayer for them all, "May They Find Peace."

I returned to my daily routine of running the station when an EMT came rushing in, threw his paperwork in the corner and exclaimed, "This job is *bullshit*! I hate this job."

"What is wrong," I asked.

"We got hassled by a chief because we were getting something to eat, eight blocks out of our area," he exclaimed.

"Don't take it personally. How many times do you actually get hassled in this job? This is the greatest job if you like patient care and making a difference," I replied.

I continued, "If you don't want to be here go do something else. Life is too short to be unhappy."

The EMT looked at me, as if he was not quite buying my answer.

I said, "Hey, you're lucky to be alive!" I nodded toward the poster on the wall and added, "Besides, I know three hundred and forty-three guys who would trade placed with you in a heartbeat."

The EMT responded saying, "Yeah. You are right, boss. That is for sure! Thanks for the perspective. You're right."

Often it is not the situation we are faced with that determines how it stresses us but how we look at a situation. I often found a way to help people see around the corner when they were pressed up against a "wall" and stressed. Changing focus or re-framing a situation a different way is the key to lasting in a career like EMS in the Bronx.

Morgue Duty Downtown.
March 2002

After I left Ground Zero and returned to my station I vowed never to go down there again. When I left I felt like I had taken ten years off my life. I never sought overtime downtown. I never wanted to go back there again.

When I reported for work one day, however, I was told I was being detailed to Ground Zero for 12 hours. The lieutenant told me I was assigned to work downtown at the morgue. I dropped my head, smiled and emphatically said, *"No way!"*

The lieutenant responded, *"Yes way*, Kanarian, it is your turn."

"Ok," I thought, "I will do my part for one day; how bad can it be?"

I called school and told them I would not be able to teach that night due to overtime. I drove to Ground Zero in my Command car. We were supposed to drive to Battalion 10 and take the shuttle but I did not want to be trapped down there like everybody else.

I parked a couple of blocks away and walked to Ground Zero. The walk reminded me of those midnight walks we took downwind. I recalled the debris and the difficulties we encountered. Now, the site was organized and clean, at least up on the streets. Down below crews were working to check for body parts and evidence.

The recovery operation was moving full speed ahead, and a lot of debris had been removed since the last time I was at Ground Zero.

The Lieutenant I was relieving said, "there are 3 EMTs, a doc and an anthropologist here under your command."

"An anthropologist?" I inquired.

He replied, "Yes, they ID the fragments as a human or animal and sort the pieces found."

"Hmm," I thought, "this is a pretty exact science. They are not looking for people anymore but identifying the parts.

I heard a voice on the radio saying, "Command to Morgue; we need a Gator in the North West corner of the pit for a removal."

Then I heard the response, "10–4 they are on the way; Gator 1 read direct heading down to the pit, North West corner.

I watched out the door as the crew drove the Gator up Church Street and then turned into the pit, disappearing in the depths. I could see the steel supports of the Trade Center with tons of debris from the upper floors jammed between them.

I wondered, "Where would Carlos Lillo be." I then thought, "Where are you?"

The pit looked like a giant trash compactor, only this pile had people and rescuers in the mix.

Parts of bodies were brought up to the morgue and tagged, "Human, "Human, rat." The rat part was flicked into a bucket for disposal; the others went to the morgue. The back of a morgue truck was filled with tagged parts that would be tested and identified through DNA.

I was hanging around in the morgue when I heard a command on the radio, "Gator to the hole forthwith."

There was a rumor Engine 777 had found a piece of a man for whom a memorial service was being held the next day. They were in a rush because now they could have a funeral for him. A leg came up with the turnout pants; a wallet was in the pocket.

Then, I heard another radio command, "Need Gator to same spot ASAP. Assemble an honor guard; found the rest of the body. No honor guard, do something Lou."

I called Command and asked for firefighters for an honor guard. Cambridge firefighters came around the bend in dress uniform. They looked like they were almost going to be sick when they saw the body torso covered with the American flag. The head had been pushed into the chest cavity.

I went to the morgue with the honor guard.

Later, I went out back to get a breather and saw the bags, small white bags.

I asked someone, "What are those for?"

He replied, "They are kids bodies bags, but we really have not had much use for them. When the Feds send disaster supplies, they send everything. You can take some if you want."

I exclaimed, "What! Using a child body bag would be bad luck; I wouldn't want to touch those."

I looked to the right and saw a pile of Scott Air Pak bottles four feet high and failed in every conceivable way. They were crushed, burned, split, and blown out. The firefighters looked dazed when they went by and saw them; their lives depended on those bottles.

Realizing the Need to Get Help
Handling Emotions

Moira called and told me she painted the pirate boat green, because that is the color paint we had in the shed.

I said, "Moira! *You stain a pirate ship; you don't paint it green.*"

Painting the boat was one of the things that had been placed on hold since 9/11, and now the wrong thing was done in her haste to do something.

As she spoke, her voice became so distant.

I thought, "I can not believe she had opted to paint the pirate ship I made for my Son Alex's fifth birthday, Green!"

The rage I felt was so pure and seething, I shut down.

I simply replied, "Fine. I have to go."

This shift at the morgue pushed me over the edge. I was scared at the lack of anger and yelling. This anger was way beyond something I could express. I felt different emotions and knew now was the time to get help.

I approached a Minister who was at Ground Zero and asked to speak with her.

I said, "I need to talk."

She replied, "Now is not the time. We are here to raise spirits and provide support. You need to seek help in a professional environment, one where you can be heard. This place is not the place to talk about emotions."

I called the Counseling Unit to request an appointment.

I asked, "Can I come by now? Or on the way home?"

The counselor replied, "No, come in on your day off."

As the counselor asked my information, my eyes began to tear and I knew I was doing the right thing, for myself. I felt relieved.

XV
The Appointment.
March 2002

When I arrived at the office for my appointment I was apprehensive about having a firemen for a counselor and discussing my feelings because of the overriding thought that EMS does not measure up to firemen. I was glad to meet with an independent counselor hired by the department to deal with issues after September 11, 2001.

When I walked in she asked me some basic questions, "What is your name?"

"Lt. Kanarian," I answered.

"Where do you work?"

I replied, "EMS Battalion 55."

"What is the phone number there?" she inquired.

I could not answer, my mouth quivered and tears streamed down my face. I tried to speak but I could not. I took a deep breath and told her the phone number.

For the remainder of the session I wept and talked about my experiences concerning September 11th and asked why it bothered me so much.

She said, "September 11th was a tragic day where many fire firefighters, EMS personnel and civilians were killed by terrorism. You're supposed to be bothered by tragic things like this."

I replied, "I mean, I have seen some horrendous things in my career. Shootings, deaths from fire and trauma. I have never experienced this level of stress. Usually we see something bad and it goes away in a couple of days."

"I see." she said and then added, "Steven, when you were working at Ground Zero your mind was recording every sight, sound, smell and thought your senses were taking in. Your autonomic nervous system protects you and helps you focus on the job at hand. After the event is when all these thoughts and information re-surface. The information was too much to process at the time, and now your mind is trying to process it with all of this sensory overload. Each moment you were down there was like those bad calls you get once or twice a year."

I said, "Oh, I understand now. It is like downloading a zipped computer file that is 10 gigabytes but your hard drive is only 9 gigabytes."

"Yes, that is one way to put it," she said in agreement.

I told her, "I came because I was wringing my hands and felt very distant."

She asked me a question and I thought for a couple of minutes, then asked, "What?" I was shaking my head trying to feel awake and told her, "I am sorry. What was the question?"

The counselor told me, "You are exhausted! It takes a lot of energy to deal with issues like this. You have a lot on your mind. Can we meet again on Thursday?"

"Yes," I replied. "That would be fine." Then I asked, "Why do I find myself wringing my hands like that?"

"You are doing that so you can feel something tangible," she replied.

I found the counseling to help me deal with issues and "see around corners." I asked her, "Why does this bother me so. I have only cried 2 or 3 times in my life. Why now?"

The counselor replied, "Each of these times has struck at the pillars of your security; made you feel vulnerable and unsafe."

"I was safe at the Trade Center," I replied.

The counselor answered, "Steven, when you work in an area in which buildings are falling from the sky you forge forward and adrenaline helps you deal with the job. Deep down inside, your mind knows that when buildings are falling from the sky the ground you walk on is not safe."

I went for a number of sessions on my own time, paying for parking and going downtown for counseling. The sessions ended abruptly when I reported for an appointment and a light duty firefighter looked up said, "Oh she is gone. She broke her ankle. She will be out six to eight weeks," and then went back to the discussion he was having with another firefighter.

"How can they be so rude and not call to cancel an appointment, or offer to re-schedule. I am done with this place," I thought.

Overall counseling helped to deal with the grief and magnitude of September 11, 2001. Often victims of PTSD feel nobody understands what they have been through. I found some counselors that were helpful at different times but found that different strategies helped with different aspects of PTSD.

A podcast that helped me relax and deal with flying anxiety was very helpful. Having someone to help me see around "brick walls" and correlate my mind's response to the stress was most helpful.

I think professionals in emergency care should develop a relationship with a health care professional and see them when stress becomes an issue.

XVI
Carlos Lillo

C arlos Lillo was one of the New York City Fire Department paramedics who died on 9/11. A memorial service was held for Carlos in March 2002. His funeral was held on September 14th, 2002. I was not able to attend the funeral because I was working that day, and other paramedics who were closer to him needed to be there. I was not too friendly with Carlos, but his death bothered me quite a bit. We worked together and I respected him. I like to remember Carlos as he was when he was alive.

My Memories of Carlos as a Colleague

I first met Carlos Lillo during a softball game in the Bronx. Jacobi EMS Station 23 had a softball team that competed against other EMS stations. I was a very good batter in baseball. I had a success in softball by hitting solid strokes over the infield and getting on base. By the end of the game the opposing team would think I was not able to hit very far. After the outfield had adjusted and moved in, I would crack the ball deep into center field for a double or triple.

One game I was up to bat and I clocked the ball hard to deep left center. The ball was heading for a depression on the field just over the edge of the horizon. I saw a player sprinting toward the ball. I ran fast to first and got ready to run to second, looking up to see where the ball was. I was stunned to see the ball streaking towards second base. I stopped at first and blurted out "Who the Hell was that?"

"That's Carlos Lillo. He's good, huh?" the first baseman replied.

"That hit is usually a triple," I remarked.

"Yep, that's Carlos," the first baseman replied while smacking his fist into the glove and walking back to his position.

When our team would play the Lenox Hill Hospital Team we would face Carlos Lillo in the outfield. I enjoyed hitting and competing against a worthy adversary.

I next worked with Carlos Lillo when I went to Queens to be the ALS coordinator. My job was to make sure the medics had the equipment, medications and continuing education credits they needed. When I was interviewed for the job Chief Kowalczy asked me what I thought of the pre-Hospital Save Award process.

I answered, "Well Chief I think it is a good award but it usually comes in a year or so later when we can't even remember the call. I have started keeping copies of call reports to keep with the save request so I can refresh my memory of the call when I get the award."

"Exactly," Chief Kowlalczyk replied, "I want to change that. What do you think would be a good time limit for that award to be processed."

"I think ten days is a good limit," I answered.

"I think that there are some other things that may pop up. I'd like to see the awards issued in one month," he said.

After I was selected for the position, I was spending time making sure the medics had their equipment and preparing Pre-Hospital Save Awards. One day Carlos Lillo came up stairs and said to me "we had a save on overtime this morning, it was a VFIB we shocked him twice and he came back with pulses. He woke up in the ER. Here is the save request. I guess we will see it in a year or so." Carlos said snidely.

As Carlos walked out of the Office and walked down the ramp to station 46 I thought, "How cool would it be to have the award done by the time he came back for his shift on tour 3?"

I looked the paper work over and began to enter the information into the mail merge file for the paramedics and EMT's on the scene.

I was careful about getting the names spelled correctly and putting the accurate shield numbers in. I called the hospital ED to confirm the patient was admitted.

I was told, "Yes he is the CCU and doing well, awake and oriented. Should be well; keep your fingers crossed. That was a good one."

"Thank you, Kathy," I replied.

I printed the certificates and letter and put them in Chief Kowalczyks' mailbox, and then I continued my work.

Later in the morning the Chief emerged from his office with the letters in hand and he smirked as he said, "You'll have to correct these; the date is wrong."

"What?" I inquired

He answered, "The date. Look the date is today for the save and the letter." The Chief had circles around the dates in red.

I replied, "Chief, that save happened this morning. Carlos Lillo was up here complaining that saves take a year. I thought it would be cool to give the save around in one day. He is a great medic; it is the least we can do for him."

The chief said, "Oh. I'm sorry. Do me a favor; re-print the letters and I will sign them."

Later I placed the saves in the mailboxes for the EMTs and paramedics on the save and went back to my office. Later in the day Carlos came into the Borough Command and quipped, "What is this? Same day service?"

"Yup," I replied.

Carlos said, "It should be like this all the time, and then he went back downstairs."

I could see he appreciated the effort but would not admit it. Recognition means something to EMS providers because we often get run down from dealing with bad situations. It is nice to receive recognition when it is deserved. A genuine "Thank You" from a patient's family will give you the motivation to keep pushing on for 3 or 4 months. Most EMT's and paramedic work for the satisfaction of helping others, the enjoyment of working with their partner but a good "Atta boy" or certificate is good once in a while.

During EMS Week 2005, Carlos Lillo was recognized as paramedic of the year by Astoria General Hospital. At a large dinner sponsored by the hospital at a local Marina, Dr. Aquino and his staff gave complements to Carlos Lillo for being medic of the year. Carlos and his partner Pat Bahnken were recognized for a stroke patient that they had treated and helped survive by aggressively caring for her.

I left the Queens Borough Command when I was promoted to Lieutenant. After being in the Bronx for a year and butting heads with my Captain, I was offered a position in Queens working on a paramedic response vehicle and doing patient care while supervising. I gladly accepted the change of management style and opportunity to care for patients again. I supervised Carlos Lillo in the Astoria Station, which was a small station where everybody respected Carlos. In the late 1990 there were not a lot of paramedics so only the best EMTs got into medic class. To be a paramedic then everybody was pretty aggressive. Carlos was not a hero or a icon; he was one of the guys who was liked by everybody. I cannot recall a bad word about him. I remember him to be quick to give a laugh during CME or in the kitchen talking to employees. Carlos and his partners were extremely close and spent weekends going out with their wives.

I can recall putting mail in employee mailboxes and seeing Carlos CME letter in his station mailbox. The continuing education letter was used every three years to demonstrate that you had attended physician lectures and call audits so you could be recertified so you could keep you job. Carlos left his letter in the open in his mailbox. To me that was a huge sign of how he trusted his co-workers and how they respected him. In those days there was a lot of camaraderie and practical jokes. If the staff thought you had wronged them, you would get your combination lock glued on your locker or come into work one day to find your locker casted with plaster. One lieutenant who was very mean to employees would often find his lunch bitten into or half-eaten as a sign of discontent.

Carlos had the respect and admiration of all his coworkers and he cared for each of them. I think it is important for people to know that Carlos Lillo was not a perfect guy; he was a great person who cared for people — patients and coworkers alike.

I spoke to Carlos Lillo's brother at a golf tournament held in honor of Carlos' memory. When I asked him if there was anything he would like future EMTs and paramedics to know about his brother he told me this story.

When they were dedicating the memorial in front of Astoria General Hospital, a homeless man came up to me and said, "Your brother was a good man; he was caring and generous. He would stop and talk to me, ask me how I was doing. And when I really needed help, he would give me some money for food."

Carlos Lillo was a good medic who knew that caring goes beyond patient care and extended to caring about people.

Pat Bahnken's Memories of His Partner and Friend

I had the opportunity to speak with Pat Bahnken, President of Local 2507 Uniform EMTs and Paramedics, about his partner, Carlos Lillo. We talked about the kind of paramedic Carlos was, and the friend that he was to Pat.

When I asked him to discuss what kind of paramedic Carlos was, Pat told me:

I was a little calmer in my approach to things. Carlos was not radical, but he was aggressive as a paramedic. He was always studying; he was always looking at new developments. He was always looking a little deeper, especially when it came to patients.

> Carlos was aggressive in that he always wanted to know more. If we brought a patient to a hospital, Carlos was never satisfied leaving that patient at the door, or leaving him or her at triage. When we'd go back, Carlos would follow up. He wanted to know if our diagnosis was correct and if our treatment was the best for the patient. Carlos was a guy that I could readily say was going to be the kind of paramedic who would take the pre-hospital care in EMS to the next level.

I asked Pat how he liked working with Carlos and he replied:

Carlos and I worked very well together. I have had

plenty of partners and I've enjoyed working with almost all of them, but there were times when I had rough periods with people I didn't get along with. When I first worked with Carlos we were kind of standoffish, but it took us only about a week or two to just find the way to work with each other. We were thick as thieves; we were tight!

It was really rewarding to work with Carlos because we would laugh; I mean we never got stressed. The job was not going to get to him. By working with Carlos, I knew the job was never going to get to me. He was a guy who always took an interest in his partners, and he took an interest in his patients. He was very excited about just life in general.

He was the kind of guy that wished he could get a 25th hour in each day. I don't know where this energy came from. Carlos was passionate about everything he did. I remember when he first started playing golf. I have been playing golf for years, but I'm not a big golfer. But Carlos, the minute he got hooked, it was his passion. I mean, it had to be golf all the time.

I remember sitting there with Carlos who liked to play soccer. So, when the World Cup was being played we had to listen to it on the radio. You know, if we were in the Battalion restocking, he was leaning into the room to watch the World Cup on television. One of the things that I truly remember about Carlos is not even about him being a medic. I remember when he first starting dating the woman who would turn out to be his wife, Cecilia. He had known her from school when he was a kid. They had parted, and hadn't seen each other in years. But by fate they got back together. They ran into each other and just hit it off. They had gone out two or three times and he'd be telling me, 'you've got to meet this girl! You've got to meet this girl!'

At 7 o'clock on a Saturday morning he drove me over to her parents' home where she lived, woke her up, brought her out of the house, still in her bathrobe. He was so excited to introduce me to Cecilia. Carlos told her, 'I want you to meet Pat; he's my partner.' I was thinking 'this poor woman, I could've met her at noon, you know.' She was just a sweet girl.

I commented, "He must have loved Cecilia, and he respected you."

Pat continued saying,

Absolutely! I mean I was very flattered, truly flattered. You spend as much time with your partner as you do with your family. In some cases you spend more time. So, you know I was very flattered that he was this excited about wanting her to meet me, but even more so, I was very excited for Carlos.

I was incredibly happy for him. It was great to see him find somebody that he clicked with so well. In that early morning meeting it became clear to me this is going to be the one. It felt great to see somebody I really cared about finally meet that person he cared about and be happy.

I interrupted Pat and said, "It seems like none of us were truly happy after September 11th. We were all walking around wondering what end is up."

Pat said, "Well, it was funny because I had seen him and Cecilia together when they got married, and they were building their house on Long Island, in Suffolk County."

I inquired, "Do you recall any outstanding jobs you worked on with Carlos?"

Pat replied:

Absolutely! I remember a couple of jobs in particular. We had several patients that had a Pontine bleed. The first patient ended up being, unfortunately, in a permanent vegetative state; he just stroked out so bad. The second guy we got with a Pontine bleed was a bleeding genesis, and we actually saved that guy. When we got there the guy was actively seizing; he was just starting to posture.

Since we had just seen two patients with Pontine bleed in the preceding weeks Carlos, being Carlos, wanted to know more about it and how it manifested and all. He was inquisitive and had a hunger for that knowledge. He started looking stuff up, getting articles, talking about it, and low and behold when the third one came up two weeks later, we were prepared.

We were so aggressive with the third patient we were on the scene in a split second. This guy collapsed at the Citibank Building in their employee gym and we had this guy in the hospital in record time. This guy walked out of the hospital. In fact, the following year Astoria General gave Carlos and me Paramedic of the Year Awards because of our treatment of that patient.

I remember that patient, but then I remember the things more importantly about Carlos. Like I said, Cecilia changed his life. When they started building their home out in Suffolk County, I can't tell you how many different paint swatches I had to look at, tiles to review, you know, fences, and windows, and carpets; I would say, "Carlos, are you going to let me live there?" I mean, he was so excited; it was great because he and Cecilia were building a life together and it was that.

I also remember his passion for golf had not waned. He was clearly addicted to the game; it appealed to him. Carlos was a very competitive sportsman. When he was in high school, he did gymnastics and he played ball.

I used to play on a softball team in Woodhall. We played against him over the years. Carlos was such an aggressive competitor. So when it came to golf, it was a game that he was playing against himself; he was competing against his primary opponent. The guy he had to beat was Carlos.

I inquired, "So, he had to be best in everything he did?"

Pat answered:

I don't know about the best. I don't think that Carlos had to be the best man on the field in anything. Carlos wanted the satisfaction of knowing that he had done the best that he possibly could. So, you know, he wasn't a man of ego; he was a man who prided himself in knowing that he had given his best effort to anything he did — whether it was patient care, golf, or softball. Anything that Carlos undertook, he undertook with a passion.

Pat went on to discuss Carlos' death, saying:

I remember it had to be the second or third night into it. Where the second night I hadn't heard. They hadn't been able to locate Carlos yet. So the department was going to send over a Chaplin and an officer to Carlos' family, to Cecilia. Much to his credit, Andy McCracken told them, 'You're sending Pat, the union is number one definitely going, and number two, Pat was his partner for a lot of years, and knows his wife. He *should* go.'

But I also remember, and it's another one of those things that I will take to my grave, going over to Carlos' apartment. We went to meet at Carlo Lillo's at 11 o'clock at night and met with Carlos' family members — with Cecilia, Carlos' mom, brother Caesar, all of them. I remember walking in and there was word that Cecilia had been laying down. She headed over to me and she just, you know, grabbed me and she was crying. I took her in my arms. It was like the life had drained out of her... Unfortunately, it wasn't going to be Chief of the Department or an EMS Chief or an officer to tell her the bad news, it was me. I told her that we had been unable to locate Carlos but had located Bobby Abril. And, based upon what we had heard, it was doubtful that we would find Carlos alive.

Pat added:

I had been president just under two years at that time. In the all the years that I have been president since then, I don't think I have had to do anything harder then to go and tell someone that their family member is gone.

Pat's Memories of Ricardo Quinn

Pat also shared some of his memories of Ricardo Quinn who was another New York City Fire Department paramedic who died on 9/11.

He said:

You know, it's funny, I knew Ricky Quinn for a lot of years too. I used to work with Ricky in Brooklyn. I remember times when we worked at shootings and stuff like that. I also remember that Ricky was an incredibly talented artist.

I also remember just as I had told Cecelia the news about Carlos' death, I repeated that message with Jamie Quinn. I remember seeing Ricky's son Kevin there.

EMS is About Caring for People

No one cares how much you know,
until they know how much you care.
— Theodore Roosevelt

The world changes at an alarming rate. Emergency medicine is constantly evolving and bringing EMS along with the medicine we represent. The supporting basis of EMS is caring for the people. Technology often tempts us to depend on computers and monitors to help patients. Medicine always comes back to the fact that technology is used to improve care, not be an obstacle between people. The best medicine is the ability to listen, the desire to help one another and the desire to help.

It has been said the patient does not care how much you know, until they know how much you care. Carlos Lillo, Ricardo Quinn, Yamel Marino and the dozens of emergency responders who died on September 11, 2001 knew this and led their lives by dedicating themselves to the unselfish service of people and their brothers and sisters they worked with.

A person who wants to make a living providing patient care should understand that people are the customer and patient care is the service we produce and deliver. Carlos Lillo lived his life knowing and demonstrating that caring for people was the most important thing.

XVII
New Beginnings.
Spring 2002

S pring arrived and the weather became warmer. Trees and shrubs in the Hudson valley started to bloom. I especially noticed the bright yellow forsythia plants that were the first to bloom in New York in the Spring. A time of new life and new beginning was upon us. Now that I was aware of how stressful 9/11 had been and how it had affected me, I decided to start bike riding to get rid of some stress and burn off the excess adrenaline coursing through my system.

I enjoyed riding my bike in the Hudson Valley. There are a lot of hills in Rockland County that present an arduous challenge. As I rode I would set goals for myself and increase my distance. I was challenged by one hill in particular on Route 9W in Bear Mountain State Park which overlooked the Hudson River. As I climbed the hill I swore to never give up. On the fourth attempt I made it up the hill all the way. As I pedaled hard a car slowed down and some teens chanted, "Go, Go, Go." I was pretty pleased to have a little support. When I made it to the top of the hill I paused to drink some water and rest. I looked out over the Hudson River and saw the nuclear plant in Westchester. I thought about the story I heard of two EMTs who were having breakfast near Perkins tower in their ambulance when the jet roared down the Hudson on 9/11. They looked at each other and asked, "What was that all about?"

I was proud of my accomplishment and decided to dedicate this bike ride to Carlos Lillo. I felt good. I felt proud to have known him and proud I did everything I could have done in the days following 9/11.

At that moment, I realized why Carlos' death bothered me so much. I had peeled through the layers of my stress and grief one-by-one. For me stress had been a series of layers like peeling an onion. Now at the center of this onion layer of grief and loss I realized that if Carlos Lillo was killed, then any of us – *including me* – could have been killed. Carlos Lillo was a great medic who was prudent. He was not a "buff" who took risks or a person who loved risk-taking.

September 11, 2001 struck at our feelings of security and invincibility as a country, as EMTs and paramedics and in our personal life as people.

XVIII
EMS Week 2002 at
St. Paul's Chapel

We take it so close to heart because we all know what it is.
Points of contention between the United States and Russia
seem like minor disputes between neighbors that fade in the
face of such great sorrow, which unites people.
> — *Valentina Nikitina, Russian economist*

A Memorial Ceremony was held to commemorate the loss of the EMTs and paramedics on September 11th during EMS Week in May 2002. On 9/11 we knew we lost eight EMTs and two paramedics who responded in ambulances as EMS professionals at the pile. As time went on, however, we realized that the deaths to EMS personnel were more widespread when the EMTs and paramedics who were working in different capacities at Ground Zero away from the pile were included.

We lost firemen like Hector Tirado who used to work at EMS Battalion 17, volunteer EMTs and Yamel Marino. It was nice to come together and remember the people we lost and mourn over the whole event as a group, together, to pay our respect.

The service was held at Saint Paul's Chapel, which is located behind the World Trade Center site in lower Manhattan. This chapel was not damaged by the falling debris from the collapse of the World

Trade Center. The history of Saint Paul's Chapel reaches back to the Revolutionary War when George Washington would rest here.

When I arrived at Saint Paul's Chapel, I saw a memorial in honor of victims of 9/11 outside. The inside design of the chapel was a colonial style wood design which was very soothing. It was a place of light and healing. During the rescue and recovery effort the chapel had served as a place of refuge, prayer and reflection.

As I entered, I saw the beautiful white interior of the church and the railing around the second level that was decorated with banners and pictures sent from around the world to support rescuers who were at Ground Zero. The walls were decorated with rainbow art and posters from kids around the country who wanted to show their support for rescuers.

9/11 Memorial Outside St. Paul's Chapel

As I walked to my seat I saw the booth used by President George Washington during his inauguration as the first President of our country. I felt proud to be a part of American history by standing tall and doing whatever was asked of me on 9/11. Even though I was never in the military, I realized I had served my country on 9/11.

I sat in the stern white wooden bench and looked around the chapel. I reflected on the event and my feeling while waiting on the wooden pew. I had attended Ricardo Quinn's funeral on September 29, 2001. Even though I had never worked with him, I went to show my respect. We were brothers because we both wore the same uniform. I felt obligated to attend this ceremony and show my respect for *all* of those who had died.

FDNY Chiefs Brown and Ianarelli at St. Paul's Chapel

I saw EMS Chiefs in dress uniform and members of the EMS honor guard. As I looked to my left I saw a group of adults and children that represented the deceased members of EMS. I wondered, "Which one was Carlos Lillo's wife? Is Chris Prescott's family is here? Chris Prescott was the first EMT whom I knew killed in the line of duty. He was killed when struck by a drunk driver from behind while he and his partner Carol Buffa were loading the stretcher into the ambulance. Although he did not die on 9/11 he was also in my thoughts.

A rabbi who spoke during the service addressed the EMS personnel who were present saying, "You are religious people. You do God's work."

His talk reminded me of one of my favorite passages from the Epistle of Saint James 2:14 in the Bible:

And one of you say to them: Go in peace, be ye warmed and filled; yet give them not those things that are necessary for the body, what shall it profit? So faith also, if it have not works, is dead in itself.

But some man will say: Thou hast faith, and I have works: show me thy faith without works; and I will show thee, by works, my faith.

Chief Daniel Nigro of the New York City Fire Department was also one of the speakers at the ceremony. He began his speech by saying, "Here we stand today as the Trade Center casts a shadow over all of us."

I thought, *"The Trade Center is gone. What is he talking about? Those towers are freaking gone!"*

Chief Nigro continued, "The World Trade Center will always cast a shadow over our minds for the rest of our lives, there is no getting over this one."

His words were the truest I have heard regarding the World Trade Center attack and post-traumatic stress. Chief Nigro's words resonated with me completely. Chief Nigro talked about the incident, the loss and how to put things in perspective. I appreciated his speech to EMS personnel given he was the fire department chief who oversaw EMS at the time. His comments were appropriate, supportive and well received.

XIX
The Master Sergeant

Transporting a Hero to the Hospital.
May 2002

I heard my unit call the dispatcher, "2–6 Frankie."

"Go ahead 26 Frank," I responded.

The dispatcher answered, "We need Conditions 5–5 here; patient is refusing to go without his wheel chair. It is an electric wheel chair that weighs two hundred pounds. We can't fit it in the ambulance."

"Conditions 5–5. Read direct. On the way," I responded.

"10–4 conditions your 10–63," the dispatcher replied.

"Driving to the call I was thinking, "What is the problem? Take the guy and the wheelchair."

I arrived at the building and knocked on the door. The door was opened by a man in his 50s. Walking slowly, the man led me to the back room.

"Are you the son," I asked?

The man turned to me, looked up and said, "Nope."

While walking into the apartment, I noticed a bookshelf that almost reached the ceiling. The bookshelf spanned the whole length of the hallway.

I realized, "Whoever lived here liked to read a lot."

The man led me to the back bedroom at the end of the hall. He pointed and said, "In there."

I walked into the room where 26 Frank and the patient were. I could see the two EMS crewmembers, Greg and Amanda. They waved and told the man, "Our boss is here now."

I said, "Hello" to the patient and then added, "Good morning Sir, what seems to be the problem?"

He answered, "Loo-tenant, come around the front of me so I can see your face."

"Shit!" I thought, "I have been here two minutes and I am already in trouble."

As I squeezed past the chair around the patient's suitcase I saw an elderly black man sitting in a wheel chair. The patient was leaning to the right a little and had a facial droop. I noticed his legs were atrophied from not being used. The patient was wearing a hat that had the words, "Korea, World War II, Vietnam" on it.

"Hi Sir. How can I help you?" I inquired.

He replied, "Loo-tenant. I just need your help to get to the bus so I can get over to the VA hospital. I have a blood problem and need to be in the hospital for five days. My doctor called yesterday. I understand this chair is heavy. I can take the bus; they have a lift."

I responded, "Sir, you should go by ambulance. I would hate to see something happen to you. We can bring you there."

Shaking his head the Master Sergeant replied, "No, No, No! I don't want to put you fella's out. These men are right; the chair is very heavy. The bus has a lift I can use."

Amanda interjected, "I am a girl."

The Master Sergeant said jokingly, "God I am glad for that ma'am. Cause I was finding you mighty cute. Maybe we should dance together one day."

"You have to catch me first, Sir," Amanda said with a laugh.

"That might be the reason I need to get out of this chair!" the patient responded.

We all have a chuckle at the Master Sergeants spirit and spunk.

Looking back I saw the patient had his military dress uniform on the coat hook of the wheel chair. I could see the rich green of the US army uniform and the hash marks for years of service. I could see his various medals and ribbons for service to our country. I saw bars above the hash marks that I had never seen before.

I wondered what this man was recognized for. "What do the bars mean?" I thought. Looking at his hat and uniform I asked the Master Sergeants, "How long where you in the military for, Sir?"

He replied, "Thirty-eight years, Loo-tenant."

I ask him, "Sir, why are you bring your dress uniform to the hospital?"

He replied, "I have marched in the Memorial Day parade every year since I retired 16 years ago. I am going to sign myself out to march this year and then return to the hospital."

I exclaimed, "Ok. We are bringing you, your chair, your uniform, your suitcase and all your friends if you want."

"What?" Greg exclaimed. "I am not lifting that chair."

I said, "Look Greg, we have spent eight months looking for pieces of people we used to work with, heroes. This guy is a living hero that gave his life to this country in service. We will take him and his chair. Period!"

"Fine, but I am not lifting that chair and wrecking my back," Greg said.

"Well he is going. I don't care if I have to call another ambulance to carry the chair. We are taking him to the VA!" I said emphatically.

We gathered the Master Sergeants belongings and headed for the door. The patient operated the chair and maneuvered past the bookshelf to the door.

"I never wanted to be in armored division but this chair is a God send, the master sergeant said.

I thought about what this man has probably been through and the energy and spunk he had. "He probably faced the Germans, the North Koreans and the Vietnamese, I guessed. These thoughts of him made me smile for the first time in a while--a long while.

We took the elevator down to the first floor and helped the Master Sergeant get his chair out of the elevator. We went out to the ambulance and opened the back doors. Greg stepped back defiantly and I looked at the situation. Amanda was about one hundred and twenty pounds and Greg did not want to help.

I said, "Oh well. Let's put him into the stretcher. As we transferred him from the chair to the stretcher I had a brainstorm.

I said, "Greg pull out two long boards, please."

Greg looked at me quizzically and then got the boards. I asked him to, "Take the boards and lay them down on the rear floor of the ambulance."

Once Greg had done that, I said, "Perfect." I aligned the wheelchair with the boards and slowly maneuvered the chair up the "ramp."

Amanda helped steady the chair. Greg and I drove the chair to the front of the patient care compartment and secured it with some straps. As I got out of the ambulance I smiled and said, "There you go Greg."

He said, "That was pretty good, boss. We got it from here."

I replied, "No, I am going to follow you guys. I don't want a complaint coming after I leave. See you at the hospital."

Slowly we rolled toward the VA hospital and pulled into the ambulance bay. We unloaded the Master Sergeant, rolled his chair down the ramp and then brought them both inside the ER. As we walked through the ER, a young man who was getting a treatment for asthma stood up from his chair and saluted and called out, "Master Sergeant!"

The Master Sergeant looked at him, straightened his head and snapped a quick salute.

I asked the young man, "Do you know this man?"

He replied, "No Sir, but I can see from his uniform he was from my unit, years ago."

I asked the man, "What are those bars for?"

"The hash marks are each for 5 yeas of service, he has seven. The bars are each for six months in active combat."

"Wow!" I exclaimed."

"Wow, indeed!" the man said, "He is a living legend."

I walked over to where the Master Sergeant had been placed on a stretcher and asked, "Are you comfortable Sir?"

He replied, "No. I would like to be home, but this will do. I have seen worse."

I said, "Sir, can I ask you a question?"

"Shoot Lieutenant," he responded.

I inquired, "What is you favorite weapon? I mean you spent so much time in the army, I am curious which is the best weapon."

The Master Sergeant leaned up and looked me in the eye, one eye drooping, the other straight at me and asked, "Personal issue or overall."

I answered, "Well, both. "

With a growl like voice he relied, "The M-1 A-1 rifle was the best weapon ever made. The M-16 ain't worth shit! My favorite all round weapon is the Bah-zooka. I could put a round in your back pocket at 300 yards."

I said, "I bet you still could do that today, Sir, Nice to meet you. Be well!"

"Thank you, Sir," the Master Sergeant responded.

I walked back out to the ER bay and I saw Greg. I helped him put the stretcher into the ambulance.

He said, "I am sorry Lou. I did not see what you saw. I only thought about getting hurt."

I responded saying, "Greg, we just did more good today than we have done in the last ten months. He is worthy of everything we can do for him."

"You're right! Thanks for helping Lieutenant," Greg added.

I got into my command car and turned on the heat. I was satisfied I had done something good. I thought, "We treated a man worthy of respect well. That's how I see it. Helping others is a way to overcome stress, or at least strike back."

Sharing Thanksgiving Dinner.
November 2003

At Battalion 55, we were trying to get back to normal — the old normal when we all brought in food and planned a nice Thanksgiving Day dinner. I had learned that if you ask people to bring in stuff they do not do it, but if you post a list of things to bring and sign yourself up first, they will follow suit and volunteer to bring things in. Everyone did.

Of course we looked forward to eating Margaret's pernil and to Judy's unique spice and baste for the turkeys, which is "off the hook."

We sat down to eat and enjoyed a nice meal. We had so much food we still had some left when we were done. As I looked around at the crew and the food, I had an idea of what to do with the extra food.

I said, "Mike, you should come with me to drop off some food. I have someone you would like to meet."

He answered, "You know we will get a call, Boss."

"I know. Why don't you come with me and Greg can go with your partner," I replied.

I got a large aluminum tray that some of the food had been brought to the station in, and we loaded some baked potatoes and yams, mashed potatoes, pernil, ham, and turkey onto it. We made another bowl with stuffing and a bag with gravy to go with the food. We had all the makings of a real All-American Thanksgiving dinner! We loaded the food into the truck and then I said, "Let's go, Mike"

Mike and I drove over to Fulton Avenue and parked the truck in front of the building. I rang the bell of apartment for the Master Sergeant but there was no answer. The landlord appeared from the side alley and said, "Can I help you? Is there a problem?"

I replied, "No. We are here to see the Master Sergeant. Can you unlock the door?"

"Sure thing," he replied.

We walked in, took the elevator to the fifth floor, walked to the apartment door and knocked.

"Whoizzit?" a voice asked.

I responded, "EMS. We are here to see the Master Sergeant."

The peephole opened a bit and then the door swung open.

The thin man who opened it said, "We didn't call no ambulance."

I told him, "We brought food for you guys. Happy Thanksgiving!"

The man backed away and opened the door and said, "Come on in then."

We walked into the back of the apartment and saw the Master Sergeant watching the parade on TV.

In his raspy voice and southern accent he asked, "Loo-tenant, what brings you boys by to see me?"

I replied, "Sir, we had some left-overs and you were the first person we thought of to give them to."

Mike placed the tray down on the table in front of the Master Sergeant. He poked at the aluminum foil and then pulled it away and exclaimed, "My gad, sweet potatoes, corn, gravy, turkey and stuffing. This is fine food, boys."

I answered, "Yes it is, Sir. There is enough for you and your buddies."

The Master Sergeant looked up and beamed. He nodded his head slightly to the side and said, I appreciate this food and your thoughts. Happy Thanksgiving boys!"

"Happy Thanksgiving to you too, Sir," Mike and I replied.

The Master Sergeant started eating turkey from the serving tray, and I began backing out of the apartment.

As Mike and I walked out the front door he exclaimed. "Man, you made his Month!"

"Really?" I asked.

"Yup!" Mike repeated, "You made his month. Did you see the look on his face?"

I answered, "I didn't pick up on it, but I am glad."

Mike and I walked back to the truck and headed to the station. I was happy I did something nice and appreciated a man who gave his life to us in service.

The Master Sergeant appreciated us bringing him the food on Thanksgiving Day far more than we ever anticipated.

I guess in a lot of ways we are all looking for appreciation from our fellow man for the things we do in our life. It is not the money or recognition we get; we all work to get the appreciation and respect of our co-workers and our fellow man. That is why we all serve and put ourselves at risk for each other.

XX
A Coincidental Event?
Spring 2003

I received a message from the dispatcher to telephone him. When I called him he said, "I need your help with this problem."

"Oh, Boy!" I thought, "here we go."

He continued, "This woman came home from the hospital and found some EMS equipment. I cannot spare a unit right now. Do you mind swinging by and picking up the equipment?"

I replied, "No, I do not mind, even though it is way out of my area."

"Thanks. You know the deal with that," the dispatcher replied.

I was sent on a call to 2001 Story Avenue, Apartment 911. As I drove over to the apartment I thought about the address. What a freak thing to be sent to this address. The woman who opened the door told me, "I came home from the hospital and found this equipment here."

I turned and looked out the window towards the South over Manhattan. I tried to place where the Twin Towers were.

"Where the Twin Towers visible from here?" I asked.

"I was standing right where you are when they fell," she replied.

"What?" I inquired.

The woman exclaimed, "I saw the whole thing from here. The

planes hit, the towers burned and then they fell on those poor people. I can hardly look that way anymore. I would rather see them in my mind and tell myself everything is the way it always was."

"No Ma'am, things are different now forever," I replied.

"They sure are, Sweety. God bless you," she added.

She squeezed my hand and I felt a rush of appreciation.

I said, "Thank you, Ma'am."

She responded, "No, thank you! Your people saved my life."

I smiled and left, slinging the O² (oxygen) bag over my shoulder.

I was amazed at my being sent to 2001 Story Avenue, Apartment 911. I thought, "This was not an accident. This was meant to be. *What is the reason?*"

I wondered, *"Why was I sent clear across the borough out of my area to this address?* Were coincidental events such as this one random or purposeful? Why had this happened? Were the events on 9/11 so crazy that we now scrutinize each item and fact until we find some meaning? Some reason."

Just as people were still looking for small fragments of bone and tissue downtown, we were all still looking for some lesson, reason or meaning for the terror attacks on the World Trade Center and the deaths of so many people — citizens, colleagues and some friends.

XXI
The Five Year Mark.
Kids in a Bus Accident

I heard the call for help over the radio, "Two-Six David calling central," the radio chirped.

The dispatcher answered, "Proceed Two-Six David. We have 14 children and 2 adults involved in a school bus accident...I need 3 more BLS and a supervisor, central; staging is located at East Tremont and Morris Park Avenue."

The short pause of radio silence was interrupted by the dispatcher saying, "Conditions 5-5, respond to the 10-32, Ground Transport Incident."

I acknowledged the assignment, "10-4, Conditions 5-5 responding."

I responded as a supervisor to this MVA (motor vehicle accident) to oversee Medical Branch Operations as dispatch began assigning units. I placed a called saying, "Two–Six Boy, Twenty Adam, I need you...."

Upon my arrival I found a small school bus involved in an MVA with a van. The bus had minor front end damage. The EMTs requesting back up were triaging 14 children as additional units were arriving. The children had minor injuries only requiring evaluation at the hospital. The biggest obstacle seemed to be packaging and transporting the children.

While tracking the patients, I was recording each patients name, age, triage status and hospital destination. EMT William Heilman began reading off the information on his patients. Their birthdays in particular stood out, "...August 15th, 2001, September 7th, 2001, September 11th, 2001 ..."

I quickly realized that these children were all 5 years old and born right around, or on, September 11th, 2001. I wondered, "How will being born around September 11th, 2001 affect these children? A happy occasion of childbirth for their mothers' was overshadowed by terrorism. How will that event affect these kids?"

I thought I was alone in thinking about the children born on September 11th, 2001. When I made a passing comment to William Heilman, however, he looked up with glassy eyes and echoed my concern saying, "That's messed up Lou. All these kids were born around 9/11."

Each of the EMT's in earshot looked up with the same distressed look. I then became aware of the skin on my arms had tightened and goose flesh had formed. In an instant September 11th was back and a very vivid memory for all of us. I realized I was not alone; the event I thought I had put behind me was still in all our minds. What seemed like a minor MVA and a routine response would evoke deep-seated emotions in all of the EMS providers on the scene. In an instant, the memory of September 11th was evoked because the children's birthdates triggered this response, even 5 years after 9/11!

While working as a paramedic in the Bronx for many years I had always thought that critical incident stress was a fallacy, something experienced by other people. However, I learned first-hand in the months following September 11th, 2001 how events can work their way in our minds and overwhelm us. The events experienced during this school bus collision 5 years after the terrorist attacks on the World Trade Center reminded me how real of an issue PTSD is.

AFTERWORD
Looking Towards the Future at the Ten Year Mark

On September 11, 2001, nearly 3,000 lives were lost in the deadliest attack on American soil in our history. We will never forget the images of planes vanishing into buildings; of photos hung by the families of the missing. We will never forget the anger and sadness we felt...the passage of time will never diminish the pain and loss forever seared in the consciousness of our nation.
— *President Barack Obama (9/11/2010)*

I have spent many years looking down at the ground trying to understand the magnitude and depth of the events of September 11, 2001. A bolt of hatred was flung from evil and struck targets in America. As Keith McGregor said, *"They took giant planes filled to the top with fuel and hundreds of people and slammed them into a densely populated area on purpose. Nobody even considered that level of insanity."* When these planes hit the World Trade Center, the Pentagon and the gound in Shanksville Pennsylvania, we were shaken from the heavens to the core of our souls and from America to all points on the globe. For me seeing a Massachusetts State Trooper and the Los Angeles County USAR team on Broadway was the most foreign feeling I have ever felt. I have seen firsthand how people are pulled together to help irrespective of color, uniform or nationality in the worst moments of our world.

Many of my co-workers try to deal with these sights, sounds and memories. Some are trying to bury these events in negative ways through denial. We all hoped time would heal the wounds and provide distance from the events we lived through. As Chief Nigro said, "There is no getting over this one." He meant September 11, 2001 is part of our souls, and part of our country's history.

The 10th Anniversary now looms on the horizon as ominously as the dust cloud raised from Ground Zero after the collapse of the Twin Towers. As we approached the 10th anniversary, I tried to find some meaning in this tragedy. I wondered, *"What could come out of such an attack in which thousands of people were killed, and one of the great American icons was destroyed. What could be said about an incident that still continues to make responders, passersby and neighbors ill from respiratory disease and cancer?"* There is no good to come out of September 11, 2001. There are no lessons learned, just lessons confirmed.

My mission was to put pieces of this event together and understand the day as much as possible. Being on the USAR team on the night shift, I was not exposed to the media information and stories of 9/11. I wanted to put the pieces together and learn what my brothers and sisters in EMS lived through. I also recognized that the events of September 11, 2001 where important to share with future EMS providers. I felt that I was in a unique position where I saw the events behind the "Pile" downtown and have had the opportunity to talk with different circles of responders because of my position as an educator. I had also worked with several of the people who died on 9/11 or perished in the months and years since and had the desire to share these stories.

When talking to Pat Bahnken, I realized that we both were respectful of those we lost, appreciated our health and had an interest in sharing the future of EMS. His quote explains why we went into harms way to try to rescue our colleagues: *"What enables cops, firefighters, EMT's and paramedics to do the job we do is the knowledge that if something does go wrong, if something happens that everyone of my brothers and sisters is going to be coming for me and knowing that they would be coming for me, obliges me to do all that I can to come for them."*

I have seen video specials about the great fires in Yosemite National Park and the forests of America. Even though hundreds of thousands of acres of land were destroyed, life returns gradually, and new grass replaces the old trees that towered above the forest. Birds are now able to eat the seeds that were previously protected by their shells. Life begins anew, scars and burn marks from the firestorm remain and will not be forgotten, evermore part of the landscape itself. But life does go on!

I have seen some trauma victims who are lucky to survive a horrendous collision. They are glad to be alive and experience life. They have deep scars that are healing; scars that will be filled with pain as they try to walk again, and muscles that will ache when it rains to remind them how lucky they are to be alive.

For me, I think we have to remember the sacrifice of those who died on 9/11 and in other tragic events. I think we have to help those who have lost people and we have to share the experiences and lessons learned from them with the new EMTs paramedics, firefighters and policemen who are going to fill the ranks and respond next time terrorism or tragedy strikes. I think they have to remember why they should be forever diligent, so we do not repeat this type of terror attack and have the high number of casualties and see another poster of innocent faces lost.

It is often said that, "That which does not kill you makes you stronger." At EMS we move forward with a clear respect for the events of September 11, 2001. Mindful of the loss and sacrifice of our brothers and sisters and appreciating the frail nature of every day. We go forward not knowing what the future will hold, but knowing that life is a gift and we can handle whatever challenges lay ahead, together.

We wondered how we would get through this event and recover. In the end I see that in the worst moments of our country we pull closer together under the pressure and unite under the flag to help not as a country of cities but as one country. Day in and day out we unite together in uniform and take pride in our departments. On the worst days in of our lives we unite under the American flag and feel closer as a country.

How do we reconcile the death of helpful EMS providers like Paramedic Carlos Lillo, Paramedic Ricardo Quinn, EMT Yamel Marino, EMT Richard Perlman, EMT Mario Santoro, Paramedic Keith Fairben, EMT David Marc Sullins, EMT Mark Schwartz and EMT Mitch Wallace and those providers who had become firefighters to enhance their ability to help people like EMT Hector Tirado, Paramedic James Pappageorge, Paramedic Andre Fletcher, EMT Joe Henry, EMT James Coyle, EMT Karl Joseph, Paramedic Kevin Pfiefer and EMT Sean Tallon of the FDNY.

I was especially impressed when I heard that because they were paramedics, Officer David Lemagne and Lt. Bob Cirri of the Port Authority Police Department responded to the World Trade Center to help people in the Towers. I have heard they were found carrying a woman up the stairs from the basement in a stair chair. We salute the actions of all these fine EMTs and paramedics for their caring, compassion and courage each day working as EMTs and paramedics. We raise our service in hopes of reaching their level of dedication. Through their example EMS will be a greater and more noble endeavor.

We go forward aware that every day is a superb day and life is an awesome gift. We move forward by enjoying life and occasionally dedicating a family moment of fun or success to one of the people we knew who have perished. We go forward especially aware of the vibrant red, white and blue colors of the American flag and how she gives us strength and unity. We move forward knowing we save lives sometimes, but have the power to heal through appreciation and caring every day.

The Downwind Walk is a story about rescuers who went into harms way and not away from it. We went downwind and that wind continues to carry us along and remind us of that day. We are forever with the downwind and the effects of that exposure continue to emerge. September 11, 2001 was not a defined one day or couple of month incident.

The aftereffects of this incident continue to emerge as new diseases in rescuers are discovered. The losses are felt every time there is a wedding where a father is not present, a holiday with loved ones missing, and graduations without parents. This is a mass casualty incident of our generation and of American history. This is why I needed to share my view of this tragedy with you, the reader.

I sincerely thank you for allowing me to do that.

APPENDIX

A Final Word with Pat Bahnken

When we finished talking about Carlos Lillo, I asked Pat Bahnken a few questions how the tragic events of 9/11 affected him in his role as our union president.

I asked, "As union president, what were your thoughts when you started hearing the numbers of people missing and presumed dead?"

Pat replied:

> There was nobody thinking about that. I remember that afternoon, that evening, we had begun locating bodies later that afternoon, and they were taking them off the Pile. I remember they would put a guy in the stokes basket and drape him with a flag and carry him out.
>
> I remember I was standing on the third floor of the Lehman Brothers Building, the atrium down there, West Street and the debris Pile was on the right. You could almost walk right out on it because the windows were all blown out. I was there with Fire Battalion Chief Nick Visconti and it was incredibly surreal. I remember looking out this window and all you saw was that it was cloudy, it was dark, and the air — all the pulverized material was hanging in the air. Nighttime was starting to become dusk, and the fires that were burning, it was like, you know,

literally, the only way I can equate it is, you know, it is what I imagined it would be like if you stood at the gates of Hell and looked in.

...I remember looking up earlier in that afternoon with Jimmy Scully and you know, Jimmy was one of those guys who was a can do guy and was like 'get it done.' I wasn't down there as a union president, I was down there as a paramedic, and we needed some stuff, you know further up front. So Jimmy commandeered a Gator; basically somebody got off it, walked away from it, and it was ours.

I commented, "Yeah. He was *balls to the walls!*"
Pat responded:

Yeah, so we went and grabbed a bunch of stuff, came back down and I, you know, little bits and pieces of that day keep coming back to me. I remember when they found Pete Ganci, Chief of the Department. He was in an ambulance on one side of the atrium. I remember his aide, I don't remember his name, he was a big guy and he was on the ambulance and Pete was gone. They were going to take him to the morgue and one of the guys said, 'Look they have Bill Feehan's body a block away; there's just no way to get there.' I remember Walter K. looked at me and he said, "Patty, do you think you can get it done?" You know, it was funny because there were a bunch of chief officers from other agencies that were debating on how this could be conducted and then Walter just turned to me and said, 'you need to get this done.'

So, Jimmy and me just disappeared. Fifteen minutes later we came walking back and you know we had a group of guys who helped us carry Billy Feehan. There was firefighters standing watch over Billy Feehan's body and there was a group of EMT's that were there in case anybody needed treatment on the Pile or whatever. There were a couple of bodies there, so I asked 'Which one is Commissioner Feehan?' and they pointed to one. Then they asked, 'Where are you going?' I said, well you know we located Chief Ganci and we took Chief Ganci to the morgue. They felt that these two gentlemen should ride together, and the guys were great, six of us went. I remember the circuit. We had to walk through the promenade, come through this glass window, walk across the debris–strewn lobby, carry the body down this escalator, and again go through a debris-strewn lobby. I mean there was like water mains, sprinklers going off, and we were just getting drenched. All six of us carried Billy and we brought him into the back of the ambulance and all these other guys were standing there and they were saying, 'What are you doing?' I said, 'We got Commissioner Feehan in here.' So while these guys were still discussing how to get it done, we got it done. Not to pat myself on the back or anything, it was just one thing that points to the difference. I don't take anything from these firefighters; they are incredibly brave men. They are giants, but they are very regimented. They have to be. It speaks volumes to them. But as paramedics and EMTs, we're expected to meet challenges independently and immediately overcome and adapt and so, while these guys are still trying to figure out the best way to get this done, a lowly EMS Lieutenant and a lowly EMS Paramedic said, 'Were getting it done." You guys form your committee, and we'll be done.

After my interview with Pat about Carlos Lillo, I wondered if connecting to the EMTs and medics in the union and the city is tiring to families or if it makes them feel proud. So, I asked Pat to share his opinion.

Pat replied:

I think it's a bit of all the above. You're proud to know that the person that you lost is a hero. You're proud to know that the person that you lost died doing something they believed in very strongly. It really brings great comfort, but then everybody talks about closure. You know, I remember when my father died we really accepted the loss and we moved forward. When my brother died, it was different. Every year on his anniversary, there is always going to be something there.

On September 11th, there is always going to be this huge memorial. On Pearl Harbor day, there's always going to be that huge memorial. So, you're incredibly proud, that if your loved one had to give their life that they gave their life in the service of their fellow man and did so courageously in the face of great danger. But then, is there ever really true closure. Understand?

I inquired, "Is there any closure with death, in general?"
Pat explained:
I believe there is. I mean the pain is always there, but you come to terms with it. Your loss is always there, but you're able to a degree to move on. There's also that part that we know generations from now September 11, 2001 will be a big part of our history.

I told Pat, "That's why I wanted to put this story together about EMS, the few us we know...Already about half of EMS personnel were probably not even there...probably weren't even in high school...So, what advice do you have for these EMT's and Medics coming down the line and saying 'Jeez, I want to be a paramedic or I want to be an EMT, but all those people died on 9-11. What chance do I have?' What suggestion would you give these EMTs and medics in the face of terrorism?

Pat replied, "In the face of terrorism? First and foremost, be smart. Use your head, trust your instinct."
I added, "We all need to know our limits."
Pat said:
Absolutely, and there is no shame in it. I tell people

all the time, there is no shame in recognizing your limitations and acting on them accordingly. But, there is shame when you deny your limitations and your failure to act upon them appropriately costs somebody else. Because, then your limitations are not just your limitations, they are now my burden.

So, you know I speak to every graduating class and one of the things I tell them is: 'This is not a job for the faint of heart. EMS is not a stepping-stone. It is not a part time gig. It is a cruel mistress and you will either be very good at this job or you will be very bad at this job. The key is to know which one you are. If you feel that you cannot do this job professionally, you need to go. Because if you don't, this cruel mistress will chew you up and leave you in shambles. This is not a profession, this is a calling, and it takes a large degree of mental toughness.'

There are people who think that I can be one cold-heartless bastard. Family members cannot understand how when other people see the carnage of a car accident or somebody they care about just drop and go into cardiac arrest, they turn away but people like me or you are walking in, we're running in.

I responded, "We're calm and purposeful!"
Pat replied:

Exactly, that's what we do. And you know, they think that we must have this thick, tough, exterior, and we don't. You have to have a degree of steel in your nerves, but like I tell these guys, it's going to happen to everybody. Somebody's going to hand you a child that's not breathing or you are going to see a kid that has been catapulted through a windshield of a car because mom and dad decided to let him stand up in the backseat rather than strap him in. You are going see innocent people get shot and killed or young kids have a sudden heart attack or some guy have a heart attack at his kitchen table. You are going to see that. And anybody that tells you that they are unmoved by those events, is either a liar or a sociopath.

I laughed and exclaimed, "We have a few of those, right?" Pat replied:

Well, how could you not be moved? But the difference is we, in our profession, must always be able to control our emotions. Whether it's the fury of wanting to grab some child abusing scumbag and pummel him, or the anger of wanting to yell or scream at the top of your lungs at some idiot parent who had their kid in their lap in the front seat, and you're trying to figure out how to intubate this pile of mush that used to be the kids face knowing that this kid is gone but you are going to do everything that you can and then some. You just want to break down and cry sometimes, but you can't. If you can't do that, then you need to leave because this job is a cruel mistress. It's a rewarding profession. I cannot see myself doing anything else. This is want I wanted to do as a kid. I loved being a paramedic. I ended up being a politician, go figure. But, I loved being a paramedic. It is a proud profession and each of us should honor that.

"Honor the people that have died doing this job the right way," I interjected.

Pat responded by saying:

Sure, you need only look at the roll call. You look at Chris Prescott, you look at Tracy Allen Lee, or Barbara Popo and Andre Lahens, you look at these guys and you look at the many men and women who have since died from cancers related to September 11th and Timmy Keller, George Ramirez and the others who are still sick.

I quipped, "Knock on wood, we're still doing good!" Pat said:

It's a true fear. I lost half a kidney to cancer so far.

Those are more shocking words than I ever wanted to hear in my life. I see people dying every day, people getting sick every day. There's a large portion of us who survived the Trade Center, who, every time we sneeze or you get a cold, get a cough, get an ache or get a pain, we wonder, 'Is it really me, just becoming an old fart or is it something deeper?' I didn't even know that I had a tumor.

I confided, "When I left Ground Zero, I said I took ten years off my life. A year later, I ws wondering, "Will I be alive in ten years?"

Pat replied:

Exactly right! You know, I think for me the impact to me personally was I think it softened me dramatically. I used to be a really hard individual. You know, as we say in the profession, I made my bones. I made my bones in the streets of East New York and Bed Sty (Bedford-Stuyvesant) during the crack wars. I was there when the blood was running in the streets, so nobody can look at me in my career and ever say, 'He never did this.' Because, I did it in the worst of all places, and I did it well.

I said, "You did it for your country, and for the City."

Pat replied, "I did it for my co-workers. I did it for my partners."

I responded, "I meant, through your military service you served this country, and through EMS you served the City."

Pat reiterated:

But in so far as EMS goes, I did it for my partners because they would do it for me. I wasn't going to let them down. But now since the Trade Center, I stand back here and I say to myself, I don't get as stressed about things anymore, you know give it up to God, whatever. I wake up today, everything else is downhill from there, and it's an easy ride. As long as I'm looking at the grass from the green side, I'm ok. I don't get as twisted about things as I used to. So, here we are now ten years later.

I think that no one could have ever envisioned that those buildings would come down. I mean, hindsight is 20/20. You know you could sit here all day long and tell me or whomever else, 'Oh we know upon reflection...' Again, no kidding! Its real easy to figure out the buildings were going to fall down after they fell down.

But, you know the one thing I don't think John Q. Public understands is how we felt when Rudy Giuliani tried to say that after we recovered the gold there and it was no longer safe for people operating the Pile so we were going to let bulldozers and cranes start ripping apart our fallen brothers and sisters. I don't think he ever got it, and it's something that I find hard to explain to people. Really, the best way to explain it is like this: What enables cops, firefighters, EMTs, and paramedics to do the job we do is the knowledge that if something does go wrong, if something happens that everyone of my brothers and sisters is going to be coming for me. And knowing that they would be coming for me, obliges me to do all that I can to come for them.

Safety Rules to Live By and Stay Alive By

by

Steven Kanarian, EMT-P, MPH

During the course of my 25 year career in New York City I have had the benefit of a vast amount of experience and specialized training. I have taken the time to assemble this list of my MCI Rules to "Live By and Stay Alive By."

Through the years I have used these rules and applied them to incidents in the news and professional journals. I have found these rules to stand up to scrutiny and would like to share them with you so you may stay safe and share them with your students and co-workers.

- Upwind for fumes; upgrade for fluid hazards
- Staging distance 1,500 feet for explosives
- No radio transmissions for bombs or suspicious packages
- Rule of Thumb – If you can't cover the scene with your thumb, you're too close
- Partially devastated buildings – beware of 2nd bomb
- Stage 2-3 times the height of the building to be outside the collapse zone
- Reassess your safety frequently
- Look for secondary attack/event
- Think of public safety personnel as a Target
- May want to delegate lookout

Use Time, Distance and Shielding to Stay Alive!

Source: http://www.downwindwalk.com

Abbreviations and Acronyms

The meaning of the abbreviations and acronyms used in the book are included when they are used for the first time. They are repeated here for the convenience of the reader.

ACRs - Ambulance Call Reports
ALS - advanced life support
BLS - basic life support
BP - blood pressure
CO - carbon monoxide
CPR - cardiopulmonary resuscitation
CSL - Cross Street Locations
defib -defibrillator
ED - emergency department
EMS - Emergency Medical Services
ESU - Emergency Services Unit
FDNY - Fire Department of New York-
FEMA - Federal Emergency Management Agency
Gator™ – Deere & Company utility vehicle
Hemocult – laboratory test for blood in stool
IV - intravenous drip
LOC- is loss of consciousness
LODI - Line of Duty Injury
mag - magnesium sulfate
MCIs - mass casualty incidents
MDT - Mobile Data Terminal

MOS - members of the service
MVA - motor vehicle accident
NYPD - New York Police Department
NYPD ESU - NYPD Emergency Services Unit
O2 - oxygen
OV - overhead ventilation
PAPD - Port Authority Police Department
Ped - pedestrian
Probies - probational firefighters
QA/I - Quality Assurance and Improvement
RCC - Resource Coordination Center
resps - respirations
RMA - refusals of medical assistance call
SOD - NYC EMS Special Operations Division
START - simple treatment and rapid triage
USAR - Urban Search And Rescue Team
VTach - ventricular tachycardia

About the Author

Steve Kanarian
(Photo by Brian Fitzgerald)

Steven Kanarian is an accomplished EMS professional with over 25 years experience. He was trained as a paramedic (EMT-P) at Northeastern University. Steve earned a Bachelor of Science (B.S.) degree in Organizational Management at Nyack College and a Masters degree in Public Health (MPH) at New York Medical College.

Steve has been a paramedic since 1984. He was a Medical Specialist with the Federal Emergency Management Agency Urban Search and Rescue (FEMA USAR) New York Task Force – 1 from 1991 to 2009. Steve has been an EMS Educator since 1994. He currently teaches paramedics at the City University of New York and LaGuardia Community College.

In 2009, Steve retired from the New York City Fire Department, EMS Command as a Lieutenant after 25 years of service. He is a freelance writer and lecturer who has published articles and given professional presentations on pre-hospital care, EMS education, supervision and MCI management topics. His published articles on EMS and management include: "Assessing the learning objectives of EMT's and paramedics responding to terrorist incidents" and "The psychological aftermath of terrorism." Steve served as Chair of the Research Committee for the National Association of EMS Educators (NAEMSE) from 2006 to 2009.

Steve's areas of specialty are paramedic education, MCI management and EMS supervision/leadership. He is available for lectures, consulting, and special projects on these topics.

A portion of the proceeds of this book will be donated to EMS providers injured on 9/11 or survivors of responders who died on 9/11.

If you have 9/11 related stories you would like to share, please e-mail me at Downwindwalk@gmail.com (Shared stories may be used in a future publication.)